WALK THE BLUE LINE

For a complete list of books by James Patterson,
as well as previews of upcoming books and more
information about the author, visit JamesPatterson.com
or find him on Facebook.

WALK THE BLUE LINE

James Patterson
and Matt Eversmann
with Chris Mooney

Little, Brown and Company

New York Boston London

Copyright © 2023 by James Patterson

Little, Brown and Company
Hachette Book Group
1290 Avenue of the Americas, New York, NY 10104
littlebrown.com

First Edition: February 2023

Little, Brown and Company is a division of Hachette Book Group, Inc. The Little, Brown name and logo are trademarks of Hachette Book Group, Inc.

The publisher is not responsible for websites (or their content) that are not owned by the publisher.

The Hachette Speakers Bureau provides a wide range of authors for speaking events. To find out more, go to hachettespeakersbureau.com or email hachettespeakers @hbgusa.com.

Little, Brown and Company books may be purchased in bulk for business, educational, or promotional use. For information, please contact your local bookseller or the Hachette Book Group Special Markets Department at special .markets@hbgusa.com.

ISBN 9780316406604 (hardcover) / 9780316530491 (large print)
LCCN 2022907350

Printing 1, 2022

LSC-H

Printed in the United States of America

CONTENTS

PART ONE:

Protect

JAKE

Jake works in a sheriff's office in the South.

I t's day one of SWAT training, which is, without a doubt, the single hardest challenge I've ever faced.

The sheriff's office developed the program in conjunction with the Navy SEALs, whose notoriously physically and mentally grueling BUD/S—Basic Underwater Demolition/SEAL—begins with a five-week physical and mental beatdown including "Hell Week."

Days, we grapple with pain-inducing fitness regimens, as well as extreme heat, cold, and sleep deprivation. Evenings, they let us go home.

That first night, I walk through the front door and start crying.

"What's the matter?" my girlfriend asks.

I tell her about my day. "And I've got to go back tomorrow and do it all over again."

I wake up the next morning, sore and tired and broken, and go back for my second day of training. *One day at a time,* I tell myself. *That's the only way I'm going to get through this, take it one day at a time.*

But I want this. I always knew I wanted to either be in the military or the police. My father was a thirty-eight-year police officer who'd been a chief for twenty-six years when he retired. A real cop's cop.

So I'm a proud second-generation cop, but I didn't want to write tickets. I didn't want to work accidents. I didn't want to take reports. I want to do the most dangerous, the coolest, the hardest and most elite job.

Joining SWAT scratches that itch for me.

The next weeks are terrible. Absolutely terrible. *Oh, my God, what have I gotten myself into?* But when I come out on the other side, I feel incredible. I've transitioned my role from street cop to full-time member of an elite, mission-focused military unit. I'm training every day with machine guns, rappelling, and fast roping—and getting paid to do it. I'm twenty-five years old.

My baptism by fire occurs when we execute a routine narcotic search warrant at an apartment complex. Our suspect lives in a ground-floor unit, and since we don't know for sure whether he's home or out, we go with a dynamic entry—speed, surprise, and violence of action, techniques we learned in SWAT training.

We breach the door with a battering ram. The lock mechanism gives way easily. I'm the first one into the apartment.

I scan the layout. Center hallway. Kitchen to my right opposite a living room area set up with a couch and TV. All three hall doors are closed.

My job is to cover my teammates while they perform a "cleanup"—systematically clearing immediate areas where suspects might hide, like behind the TV, underneath a couch, even inside the refrigerator.

The living room and kitchen clear, my teammates burst into a bedroom. From my covering position in the hallway, I hear one of them shout, *"Heads up, we've got a dog!"*

From the corner of my eye, I see what looks like a big, muscular pit bull. I hold my focus on the two unopened doors—the one inches from my face, and the one in the center of the hallway—

Bang-bang-bang, and the doorjamb splinters in three areas. My dumb ass thinks my teammates are shooting at the dog. The thing must be aggressive as hell, but still.

"Watch your sights," I say.

"That ain't us, bro," someone replies.

Then it hits me—hits *us.* Someone is behind that door, armed with a weapon. Could be one person in there, two, maybe more. We have no way of knowing.

We came here to secure dope, not get cops killed—which is why our team leader immediately orders us to a fallback position.

"Mission has changed," he tells us. "We've got other tools we can deploy."

Because we have at least one armed suspect, we set up a barricade protocol. The first step is to evacuate the nearest apartments as discreetly as possible. Then we get on the bullhorn, ordering the neighbors outside the evacuation area to stay in their homes.

We start negotiating with the shooter.

He doesn't respond.

Bystanders do. They film the exchange with their phones.

A remote-controlled robot carries a pair of explosive devices into the apartment and affixes them to the two interior doors that remain closed. After the robot leaves, we detonate the devices. The overpressure of the explosive breach blows the doors open.

More shots are fired from inside the apartment.

The shooter thinks we're still in there.

A woman carrying a baby leaves the apartment, followed by a second guy. We're on them quickly. They tell us there's one more person in there. He's armed with an AK-47.

Finally, the shooter surrenders. We quickly discover why.

His AK malfunctioned.

The dog ran out of the apartment, unharmed.

Our goal is to always end the situation peacefully, to use whatever methods we can to get the suspect to surrender, and then safely remove him or her from the situation.

In the days that follow, people keep asking me what it was like, getting into a gunfight. "It's not like the movies," I say. "It's sensory overload. All I knew for certain is that bullets were flying everywhere."

"You should have sprayed that door with your rifle," some people say.

Everybody's got an opinion on what law enforcement should be doing. And I'm like, "Man, if they got all the answers, we're always taking applications."

What they don't understand is that we're accountable for every round we send downrange. That if I haven't positively identified a target—including the suspect—I can't shoot. That there's a potential lawsuit attached to every single bullet.

"Oh, man, you're a full-time SWAT, that must be terrifying," people say to me.

My response is always to highlight the strength of my team. "I'm going in with a bunch of guys who are just as highly trained as I am, with the best equipment, with all of our tools and technology and a lot of knowledge about what we're about to get into," I tell them. My colleagues who are by themselves and stop a car for a taillight out at 3 a.m., with no clue what they're getting into and backup is at least a radio call away? All things considered, I think that's a more dangerous job.

Now I'm working to train other guys in SWAT, and we want thinkers, not just tough guys. We want tough guys who can reason.

People might think they want cops who aren't influenced emotionally, cops who do their jobs like robots. But when you're stopped on the way to the hospital, speeding to say good-bye to your grandmother who's dying, you don't want a robot. You want somebody who's going to identify with your situation emotionally.

You want a human.

"We always operate off of safety priorities and priorities of life," our team leader drills into us. "As for the person you're dealing with, you'll never know what he or she is willing to do that day, what their compliance level is, so your situational awareness has always got to be on point."

As for the sensory overload I experienced, it takes a lot of exposure to those situations and circumstances before you start to develop some clarity and tactical maturity, I learn.

Where are we at in the priorities of life here or the safety priorities? I constantly assess in any situation. Hostages come first, because they're not free to leave the situation. Next are innocent civilians, people we need to evacuate. Then it's protecting ourselves, the first responders, from harm. We're going to do whatever's safest for us. The suspects are on the list, too, which most people forget. Most people think that we don't regard their lives. We do. Our goal is always to get them out safely as well if we can.

The shooter on that first mission, I find out, was lying underneath a bed, the AK aimed at the door. He was just waiting for us to knock it down or blow it open. If we did that, he would have easily killed the first four or five guys who came through that choke point.

And I would have been one of the casualties.

Up until this moment, I'd thought all of PT and training was fun and cool. That's when the sobering realization sinks in, and it chilled me to the bone.

I can get killed doing this.

JOCK CONDON

Jock Condon is originally from Scotland. He was a police officer in the UK and an MP in the Royal Air Force. Jock works for a sheriff's office in the Midwest.

I t's two o'clock in the morning and pouring rain. I'm sitting alone in my squad car, in the Dollar General parking lot, when a call comes over the radio about an aggravated burglary in progress. Dispatch is currently on the phone with the homeowners, a married couple.

The address is right around the corner from my location. I pull out of the parking lot. I don't hit the sirens. I don't want to announce my arrival to the intruder or intruders.

The home's porch light is off, the windows dark. As I get out of the car—

Bang-bang.

I grab my radio. "Shots fired from inside the house. I'm going in."

I'm on my own. Even if they run balls to the wall, my nearest backups are probably six minutes away.

I can't wait that long.

I draw my weapon and try the front door. It's unlocked.

Did the homeowner shoot the intruder? Or is it the other way around?

All I know is that someone inside the house has a gun.

I open the door. As I step into a dark living room, my thoughts turn to the extremely sticky situations I got into over in Afghanistan, serving with the British Diplomatic Security teams. Somehow, I not only managed to survive but to return home in one piece. Tonight, I'm gripped with the feeling that my luck is about to run out.

I fall back on my military and police training and start "slicing the pie," a well-tested and essential battle tactic for assessing choke points where a shooter could be lying in wait.

The living room is clear, but I have no idea where the homeowners are, what they look like.

I can hear radio traffic over my earpiece, but I tune out the words and focus on my surroundings. The living room leads into a kitchen. I approach cautiously, certain that I'm about to engage in close-quarters combat.

My priority is the safety of the homeowners. It's counter-intuitive to me personally but from my training, I have to take the risk. I announce myself as loudly as possible.

"Homeowner! Sheriff's office!"

I move to the gap between where the living room meets

the kitchen, certain that a muzzle flash is going to be the last thing I see before I die. I don't have a choice. It *has* to be done. This is what cops do.

I round the corner and slice the pie, thinking of my four-year-old son tucked in his bed, asleep; thinking of him waking up tomorrow without a father.

"Don't let me die!" someone groans. "Please, God, don't let me die."

A short hallway leads to a Jack and Jill bathroom. The bathroom door is open about a foot and, lying on the floor, I see a guy who looks like Santa Claus—chubby, with a big, unkempt white beard. Santa has a sucking chest wound.

We're taught to always look at the hands. Santa is holding something small and shiny. I'm too far away to make out what it is.

"Homeowner! Identify yourself!"

"In here." A male voice. "I'm in the bedroom."

A sliver of light shines from beneath what appears to be a half-opened bedroom door on my left. I can't see who's talking, not without giving away my position.

"Who else is in there with you?"

"My wife," the man responds. "She called 911."

"Anyone else in the house?"

"No, sir," he replies. "Just that man in the bathroom."

"Put your gun down on the floor."

A beat, and then he says, "Okay. I'm no longer armed."

What if he's lying? What if the guy lying on the bathroom floor is the homeowner? I could be walking into a trap.

Santa is dying. The guy has seconds to live. If he is, in fact, the homeowner, I have to save him. If he's the bad guy,

I still have to save him. Either way, I don't have a choice, and I can't wait. I have to "do it live," as we say. To move through the choke point.

Going into the unknown, being willing to die and leave everything behind—this is the job.

Using my thumb, I turn on the tactical light attached to my service weapon. I advance slowly, dividing my attention between Santa's hands and the blind area to my left, the bedroom. I can't stop thinking about my son. If I'm going to die tonight, my last thoughts will be of him.

A quick look inside the bedroom and I see a couple in their early thirties. They're cowering in fear. A weapon is lying on top of the bed instead of the floor. The man has a look of sheer horror—the shell-shocked expression of someone who didn't want to pull the trigger and was forced to do it.

Back to Santa. The shiny object in his hands is a small metal flashlight, the kind that attaches to a key chain. In addition to a sucking chest wound, he's been shot through the face, throat, neck, and jaw.

My military experience includes treating chest injuries. When I moved through the kitchen, I remembered seeing tea towels hanging on the handle of the oven. I holster my weapon and retrieve the towels. When I return, Santa is in the grips of a "death rattle." He can't cough or swallow the saliva that has built up in the back of his throat.

I manage to keep Santa alive until the medics arrive, which includes sticking my finger into the bullet hole in his chest to seal it. Fortunately for him, the medics are located three hundred yards down the road.

The medics need more room to work on him, so they

drag him by his boots into the kitchen, leaving a long bloody smear across the floor. As they put chest seals on his entry and exit wounds, more of my team members arrive.

"I booked it over here," my buddy Jake tells me. "We thought you'd been shot."

I look at him, confused.

"The wife was on the phone with dispatch," he says. "She said her husband just shot someone. We tried raising you on the radio, but you didn't answer so we all drove like maniacs, thinking you'd been hit."

Santa is whisked away to the hospital. I have to wait for CSI and the detectives. I sit down with the homeowners. They're literally in shock. They've watched us work on the intruder, watched us drag him away. There's blood everywhere.

"I didn't want to shoot him," the husband says. "I kept telling him to get out, get out, but he wouldn't listen."

The man is despondent about having pulled the trigger. It's a big responsibility to bear. I know, from personal experience, what he's going through.

Later, I learn that the intruder will live. I also find out that Santa is an alcoholic who'd been on the wagon for years. Tonight, he decided to jump off with both feet, got as drunk as a skunk, and simply walked into the wrong house.

I was born in Scotland and raised by my father in a pretty crappy neighborhood on the country's west coast. When I was thirteen, we had trouble with our neighbors—they broke our windows, threatened us. I remember living in constant fear.

A local cop learns what's happening, grabs the head of the

family, and says, "That man and his son are friends of mine. If you keep going like this, I'm going to make your life a living hell."

That cop keeps me on the straight and narrow. By my teenage years, most of my friends are junkies, in jail, or dead. He shows me the importance of looking out for my mind and body. I go to work for an electronics company and practice kickboxing at a high level. One day I run into him and announce, "I want to be a cop."

"If this is what you want to do, then join the military and get some life experience first."

I take his advice and enter the Royal Air Force, where I serve as an MP. After seven and a half years, I leave and go work as a police officer in a university town for another six years. Then a stint with British Diplomatic Security teams, which leads to three years on the front lines of Afghanistan.

I lose my two best friends while overseas.

When I return home to the UK, I start drinking a lot. Until I'm numb. I engage in risky behavior—driving too fast, picking up girls at bars. One day I have a moment of clarity. *This isn't me. I need to move on with my life.*

I get married to an American woman. I move to the US, and we have a child. I enter the police academy and train to become an American officer. The learning curve is steep. It was still putting a uniform on and doing the job, but it was completely different, tough to get my head around a little bit.

The feeling I had entering the dark house on that rainy night—I was sure that my luck had run out. That I was going to get shot.

The guys at the police station have a different take. "Man, I've been waiting years for that type of action," they say to me the next day, freely admitting their jealousy of my "dream call." "You're so lucky."

I keep thinking about karma. How, in Afghanistan, sometimes we'd take a right turn when, if we had gone left, we would have driven over an IED at the side of the road.

You can ride your luck only so many times.

Seven months before I entered that house, I responded to a call on a cold, dark night in November. A car had collided with a deer and the animal was dying. Because it was nighttime, the animal control officer wasn't on duty, so it was up to me to put the animal down.

As I pulled the trigger, I'm back in Afghanistan, feeling the 120-degree heat, the air smelling like boiled shit. I stand on a roof, looking down the rifle scope at a Taliban fighter holding an AK-47.

No, I think, staring at the dead deer. *This isn't happening. This is not happening.*

But it did happen. And I know it's going to happen again.

And again.

This isn't my first flashback.

I'm nowhere near suicidal or homicidal, but I'm starting to understand how people get there.

My first instinct is to run from my problems, the way I've always done. But I have a wife and a kid now.

I'm very good at compartmentalizing, but I know I suffer from trauma. My wife knows it, too.

"You've been dealing with this for years," she says. "You need to confront it head-on."

I decide to confide in a county deputy who's also a good friend. Once I overcome my fear and shame and pick up the phone, I tell my friend everything.

He sends me to a lieutenant. "He's a good dude, he'll hook you up."

I call and meet the lieutenant in his office.

"I've seen some shit, I've done some shit," I tell him. "Things are catching up with me, and I need help."

He recommends a psychologist, the go-to person for local law enforcement. The next day I'm sitting in her office. I tell her about shooting the deer and the flashback that followed. Then I tell her about Afghanistan.

"I'm broken," I say. "I know I'm broken. I've tried to fix this, and you can't fix it, either. I'm damaged."

She looks me in the eye and says, "You have PTSD."

Hearing her say it out loud hits home. Part of me is relieved while another part says, *Oh, crap, I've got PTSD.*

"Look at PTSD as weight," she says. "If you're carrying, say, five pounds, you can fix that. If you're carrying five hundred pounds, you'll die. How much weight do you think you're carrying?"

"About three hundred and fifty pounds."

"Therapy and medication will help you drop that mental weight."

Now I help other cops like me. I work with our peer support groups and with veterans in crisis, try to pay forward my hard-won insight.

Asking for help is empowering. It makes you stronger. More respected, not less.

If you don't ask for help, sometimes there's no coming back.

And everyone deserves a chance to make it back.

I want to be out where people can see me. That's part of my job. I'm on the line. And I ain't going anywhere. 'Cause I'll tell you something—if your kid's in trouble, I want them to run to a cop. I don't want them to run anywhere else. I want them to run to a cop, because we will help them.

I'm just going to keep doing what I'm doing. I've got awards up the yin-yang. I've got the Medal of Valor. They look cool and everything, but no, it's the personalization of when somebody looks you in the face and says *Thank you*. And you can see that they absolutely mean it. And it's from the heart. That is the best thing ever.

Nobody hates bad cops more than good cops. They make our jobs harder. We don't want them. Don't ever put me in that position because not only will I throw you under the bus, I'll drive the bus.

I will always stand there. I bleed blue.

TARA DAWE

Tara Dawe is a veteran of the New York City Police Department.

An assignment to Manhattan's Warrant Squad means you're on track to become a detective. I'm starting there as a "white shield"—a patrolman with only a few years of experience—so I'm given low-level warrants like summons and misdemeanors.

If I do well, I can work my way up to felonies and then the prestigious hard-core WOW team, a.k.a. Worst of the Worst. Violent felony warrants for extremely dangerous and difficult-to-track-down offenders.

Everyone in the squad has their own mailbox. When I open mine, I find that I have fifteen new warrants—single sheets of paper containing each subject's information and photo. We take each warrant seriously. Warrant officers have been shot at, assaulted, or injured. You never know what the subject did the night before, never know what he or she is thinking when you show up at their doorstep. And no matter how small the violation, these people are never happy to see us.

We typically work in teams of four, for safety. When I'm assigned my team for the day, I turn to another member. "How many do you have?"

"Eight."

There's no way we can get to all our locations in one day. First, we have to find the subjects, who tend to move around. Subjects don't want to be found, and will often resort to extreme, dangerous, and even stupid tactics to avoid capture.

When we're going into an apartment building or a house, we position two people at the front door and another near a stairwell, or—depending on the apartment's location—near a roof. A fourth person stands watch outside the subject's window so he or she doesn't try to jump out.

It happens. A lot.

Once, while I was at a residence to make an arrest on a warrant for a violation of an order of protection, a man jumped out the third-story window of a brownstone. I ran down the stairs and out the front door. The subject had only made it about five feet because his ankle was busted up. Hoping I wouldn't recognize him, he pointed down the street and said, "He ran that way!"

"Was it really worth it?" I said to him after I called an ambulance. "Now you're going to be in severe pain at a hospital, and you're *still* being apprehended on the open warrant."

Social media hadn't taken off yet when I started on the job. Still, I needed to learn how to use computers and investigative techniques to find information quickly.

It's fun. I enjoy the thrill of the hunt.

Including our backlog, we have a total of forty subjects. Based on our research, we strategize and pick our top three, people we're sure we can find if everything goes according to plan. The volume of warrants is overwhelming, but we work hard to investigate each and every one.

Our first stop is an apartment in the Bronx, to serve a misdemeanor summons warrant to a man named Barry. Our research shows he's living there with his girlfriend.

I approach the apartment with another warrant officer named Tina. She's a good person but rough around the edges. When it comes to the job, she's had a tough career and has become disgruntled, even negative. She tends to see the worst in people.

As a female in a physically demanding career field, I feel like I'm a realist. I know my strengths and weaknesses. I know that if I hold my own and give 150 percent in everything I do, I'll get treated well. But if I act all tough and can't back it up with action, then I'll get treated accordingly.

I knock on the door. The girlfriend answers, says Barry isn't home. We search the apartment and find Barry hanging from a windowsill.

He's completely naked.

I shake my head. I'm here with a warrant for a misdemeanor, and this guy is acting like he's the world's most wanted fugitive.

"Are you crazy?" I say to him as Tina and I pull him back into the apartment. "You're five stories up."

His actions make me suspect he has possibly committed a more serious crime. Something we haven't discovered yet.

Occasionally, the guys we deal with don't hesitate to fight because I'm female and not seen as a threat. Barry, fortunately, doesn't put up a fight. We apprehend him, then as protocol dictates, we immediately return the subject directly to court.

Our next subject, a nineteen-year-old woman wanted for a misdemeanor Criminal Possession of Controlled Substance (CPCS) warrant, lives in a housing project in Brooklyn with her boyfriend and kids. Her seventeen-year-old boyfriend says she's not here. We search the apartment.

All my years on the job, I can count on one hand the number of homes I've entered that are filled with love. This isn't one of them.

There are no sheets on the toddler's bed. The oldest, who is five, sleeps on a mattress on a floor. I don't see a single toy anywhere, and there's barely any food in the refrigerator or the cupboards. The father is wearing $300 sneakers and has a brand-new iPhone.

The five-year-old glares at me with hatred. Doing this job, you see the same repeat offenders, get to know their families. The neighborhoods. You see kids as they grow up. It usually doesn't turn out well for them. I look at the five-year-old with compassion, hoping I won't see him down the road, a warrant in my hand.

It wears on you, though, this hatred directed at you, day after day.

The last stop is back in the Bronx. The subject, Chris, is wanted for a misdemeanor assault. He's six foot four and weighs close to three hundred pounds.

Tina bangs on the door, shouts, *"Open up!"*

"That guy opens the door, one punch to me, one punch to you, we're down the stairs," I say, moving closer to Tina. "Can you please just stop and let me kill him with kindness? Let me just placate the situation?"

The door opens. It's the subject, Chris, and he's huge.

Pissed off.

I begin my spiel, try to kill him with kindness as I explain that his situation isn't that serious. As I talk, I'm fully aware that if I get into a full-blown fight with him, most likely I'm not going to win. I remind myself that I can always come back with more people and get this guy tomorrow. My goal, each and every day, is to go home to my family and friends in one piece. I'm five nine, in good shape and bigger than most of the women I work with, but I would still have to call for backup and hope I'm strong enough to hold Chris off for as long as I possibly could until somebody can assist us. Using words to de-escalate a situation is always ideal. No cop wants a physical altercation.

My speech works. Chris relaxes, nods, and complies.

I end up getting my gold shield—Detective Third Grade—in the Manhattan Warrant Squad.

My time in the NYPD Warrant Squad is a fascinating and life-changing experience. From people jumping out windows, rolling up in pullout couches, or hiding in their kid's bedroom while the child was still sleeping—all these incidents have a lasting impact on me.

After working with the WOW teams, I can say that I will always consider them truly the bravest guys I have ever had the pleasure of knowing.

I take a position as the special projects sergeant for the NYPD's Gun Violence Suppression Division, which focuses on identifying and dismantling people and organizations that traffic and sell illegal firearms. GVSD also works to investigate gun violence and gang-related shootings throughout the city. My role is to do a little bit of everything. Mainly, I verify arrests and statistics regarding our takedown operations.

Watching the detectives in GVSD work is incredible. I'm in awe of them. NYPD has recruited the best of the best.

It was always a battle back in the day. Every division had their own sets of goals to achieve. Narcotics focused on drugs. Gang focused on the gang members and gang crime. And then you had Homicide focusing on homicide. But this new division that they just keep expanding within the police department and the Detective Bureau is tying every single thing in together into one big well-oiled machine. And I really think that's going to be the way the future goes.

And maybe it could effect some good change in these communities, you know?

We have a Joint Firearms Task Force that works with the ATF to target gun dealers. With advances in technology, we now have cameras on every single street. If a shooting occurs, footage is available from various angles. Our computer programs are sophisticated, and we can trace the sales of firearms to locations all over the country.

Yet a lot of the time, these guys are telling on themselves. Social media is everything.

One guy we arrest says, "That gun isn't mine."

A detective says, "Here are fifteen photos of you posing with that gun on Facebook."

The number of guns we take off the streets is insane. What's even crazier is that gangs are putting weapons into the hands of twelve- to fourteen-year-olds, and having them do the drug deals—because if they get arrested as juveniles, they won't get any serious time.

Back in the day, gang members were a little older. Now, they're all young teenagers or even preteens, ninth and tenth graders being charged with murder. Walking into these homes and seeing how these kids turned hardened criminals, killing one another—it tears me up. Tears *us* up.

These kids never stood a chance. Never had a stable upbringing, or in many situations, love from both a mother and father. Never woke up to pancakes on Christmas morning or had someone read them bedtime stories. No care, no love, no nothing.

It destroys a child to get nothing from a parent. When you don't get what you need at home you look for it elsewhere, and sometimes in the wrong places.

I see the unimaginable, every single day.

I'd see these young teenagers and feel such compassion for them—and then the next day it's like these same kids are mouthing off to me and one's spitting at me. I'd look at them as just a pure criminal and feel nothing. And then I reel myself back in, and remind myself, "No." I was like, "This is the same kid that I felt bad for yesterday."

A lot of people hate cops for the wrong reasons. They don't truly understand everything that we do. Almost every cop I know—Black, white, Asian, everything, male and female—we're all good people who go out every day and are really affected by the things we see and do. We really want to put bad guys away. We really want to help victims.

TIM O'BRIEN

Tim O'Brien was working in the mortgage industry when, at thirty, he decided to become a police officer.

I approach the car and say, "Do you know why I pulled you over?"

The guy behind the wheel doesn't know what to say. It's 6 a.m., and he's dressed for work.

"I was speeding?" he asks.

"No."

"Are my stickers expired?"

"No."

"Are my taillights out?"

"No. License and registration, please."

One of the essentials of police work is learning to use your discretion—when you can, and can't, arrest someone. When you can write a ticket or write a warning.

I run the guy's name through the computer. He's clean, not even a parking ticket.

I can hammer this guy with a $300 ticket, or I can let him go with a warning.

I return to the guy's car. "You went through a stop sign— that's why I pulled you over." I hand him a written warning. "Slow down, you're in a school zone."

I try to be more commonsense than hard-nosed.

I always patterned myself on the guys who didn't make a million car stops or a million arrests, but the ones they made were always good. They were always the ones that bore fruit, that led to something else.

You can read the handbook as much as you want, but I always thought back to these guys and my instructors at the academy saying, "Yeah, we can teach you this stuff, but you're going to have to figure it out. You're going to have to use common sense. You're going to have to use your life experience."

There's going to be times where you get your ass kicked or you get chewed out by management or senior-level staff, or there's calls you wish you could've handled differently or things you could've done differently. I always just try to look at it like, did I do what I thought was the right thing to do? I'm fine as long as I can answer that question and say, "Yeah, you know what? I think I did."

That's where being a little bit older helped me, I think. I went into the mortgage business, but I never forgot about wanting to be a police officer. I took the civil service exam one last time when I was almost thirty, and soon after, I hear that the little town south of Boston where my wife and I were living has an opening for a police officer.

Should I even do this? I'm getting older, I'm married, I have kids. But then I decided, *Screw it. I've always wanted to do this.*

The day of the interview turns out to be the same day my wife goes into labor with our third kid. I was hired on the way into Boston. I got a phone call from my neighbor saying, "Congratulations, you're a cop."

"That's great," I say, "I'm on the expressway heading into Boston to see my son being born."

When I was growing up in Boston, everyone I knew either had law enforcement in their family, or the fire department. One of the guys' older brothers became a priest. Some of the guys are lawyers and judges now. But almost everyone was on a civil service track—something involved in the community.

I'm a small cog, a local cop in a small town, just excited to do the job and lucky enough to do it.

I have four kids, and they all drive. I tell them, "Listen, you're going to get tickets, it's going to happen. It sucks. Maybe you'll get lucky. But if I ever hear that you're disrespectful or a wiseass or anything like that, you're going to wish they towed your car. Your mother and I won't put up with that."

It's near dinnertime and I'm at my mother-in-law's house, waiting for my wife and kids, when my phone rings. It's a cop I know from my town.

"Tim, I just pulled over a car. The driver was a junior operator."

My son is a junior operator, which means, basically, a limitation during the first six months holding the license: no kids in the car.

I'm thinking the worst when the cop says, "There were five kids in the car, and one of them was your son. He wasn't the driver. I'm calling because I wanted to let you know your kid was really nice, very respectful."

Fifteen minutes later, I get a call from the same cop. "Tim, I just pulled over your wife and daughter for speeding on the same road your son was on. What is this, O'Brien day?"

"I am so sorry."

"Do you have any more relatives on the road today? Anyone else I should be looking out for?" He can't stop laughing.

LOUIE AGUILERA

Louie Aguilera is an investigator with the Los Angeles County Sheriff's Department's Homicide Bureau.

I'm standing on the corner with my neighborhood friends when the ice cream truck comes to a stop about forty or fifty yards away. The ice cream jingle echoes through the streets as three local gang members, young guys, run to the truck, open the back door, and rush inside.

I hear a gunshot.

Watch as the men run from the truck.

I want to run after them.

I'm nine years old.

The men, I find out quickly, robbed the owner and killed him. That night and in the days and weeks that follow, I can't stop thinking that trying to support his family got the ice cream man killed.

My neighborhood turns out gangsters. Growing up here, your goal isn't to become a doctor, a psychologist, a teacher—it's to become a pro athlete, get rich, and move out of the neighborhood.

I enjoy sports, martial arts, and boxing, but I'm never going to be a pro athlete.

Seeing what happened to the ice cream man, I know right then I want to become a deputy sheriff, a gang detective. I want to work for that department that patrolled my neighborhood. I want to get gang members off the streets, prevent them from harming people. But if they do, I want to investigate homicide cases.

I become a deputy sheriff the day I turn twenty-one.

Working the streets takes a combination of book smarts and street smarts. You also have to know how to carry yourself, how to develop relationships with the people in the community you serve.

On patrol, I focus all of my energy on the local gangs, building a good rapport with them. I grew up with these guys, know how they think and what makes them tick, and the conversations I have with them help me cultivate informants from each gang. I also take Polaroid photos of gang members and the cars they drive and put that, along with any personal information I uncover about them, into a notebook.

I'm able to work a lot of cases involving gangs. I transition to South Central, Los Angeles, to a gang unit that assists homicide detectives in gang-related murders.

When you work gang neighborhoods, you don't see a lot of kids on the streets anymore. You won't see kids playing ball in the park or shooting baskets in the front of their house. No teenage boys playing out in the streets where they become targets, even when they aren't gang members.

My first night on call, around 11 p.m., a sixteen-year-old male gets shot in a residential neighborhood in Baldwin Park.

I've been around shooting scenes. There's always an aura when someone's been killed. You can feel it in the air.

By the time a homicide investigator arrives, usually two hours after the murder has occurred, the emotions have mostly calmed down. Most neighborhood spectators have gone on their way, leaving police officers to man their posts around the crime-scene tape.

Tonight, the fifty or so people outside the tape are not causing any problems with the Baldwin Park police officers, but they're hysterical with grief.

What's going on?

The sixteen-year-old, I find out, doesn't live in Baldwin Park. His name is Darryl, and he lives with his mother in a home his father owns in Corona, which is a pretty nice neighborhood. The parents are divorced, with an every-other-weekend custody agreement.

Darryl was standing outside in the front yard, talking to two friends his age, when a car rolled up. What happened next was your classic gangster drive-by—shots were fired. Everyone ran. Darryl took a shot in the back, and it blew his heart out. He died on a couch in the backyard.

One of the friends with Darryl was wearing a black baseball

cap, and in this neighborhood, could've passed for a rival gang member. That's the reason they were shot at.

Darryl wasn't a gang member. He was just a nice high school kid in the wrong place at the wrong time. The group of fifty people here are aunts, uncles, and cousins.

When I'm at a scene, I don't get very emotional because I'm processing details, trying to locate potential evidence—and when I find it, I'm constantly wracking my brain.

Today we recover very little evidence. The gun used in the shooting was a .22. We have a description of the vehicle and nothing else.

When the coroner arrives, the parents ask if they can see their son before he's loaded into the transport van.

The coroner unzips the body bag so the parents can see their child's face.

The crying from the mom and dad and the other family members, the hurt that they're feeling, tears me apart.

And fuels me.

I don't need motivation because I feel for every single victim I encounter. There's an old saying, "We don't choose our victims. Our victims are our victims." I don't care if the victim's a drug dealer, gang member, prostitute, whatever. I want to find justice for them all.

When I come home from a homicide scene, my wife and kids are always supportive. But I have so many case details running through my head that I'm too impatient to sit and talk.

I work the case. My thoughts are in constant motion, wondering what I need to do—what I can do.

Days turn into weeks and then months.

I keep Post-its next to the bed for when I wake up in a panic at three in the morning, thinking I forgot a key point, or maybe made a mistake. When I know I'm not going to be able to go back to sleep, sometimes I head to the office. I work out religiously, to the point of obsession.

We find the car used in the drive-by. It's a stolen vehicle. Inside are shell casings that match the casings we collected from the street.

When the gang member we suspect of the shooting is arrested, he's carrying a .22-caliber handgun. We send it in for testing.

It's the same weapon used in the drive-by.

When it comes to gangs, there's no such thing as loyalty. The moment they come into custody, each one always says to me, "Hey, Aguilera, who's the snitch? Who's telling on us?"

My answer is always the same. "All of you are. None of you like to be sitting in jail, so you all tell on each other, do everything you can to get out of jail."

The gang member we've arrested confesses to the crime when we're interviewing him. He and the driver both admit to the shooting, and they both end up getting a hundred years.

I've developed a close friendship with Darryl's family. They thank me for providing closure.

But I'm not providing them closure, which is a word I never use, because holidays and birthdays are going to come, and Darryl won't be there. And at each holiday and birthday, the family's wound is reopened, again and again. I can give them answers, and I can give justice, but families and friends of victims will never have closure.

What a lot of people don't realize is that we stay in contact with these families for years. You have to be there for them. You're their advocate. I tell them to call me or text me anytime. For a lot of family members, we stay in contact because in some strange way, I'm part of that victim to them.

You become a part of that victim, in each and every one of your cases.

On a Friday night, I'm watching the news when a reporter breaks in live with a story about the search for a five-year-old boy in Arroyo Seco Park in South Pasadena. The father is found passed out near his car. He's alive but has no idea where he left his kid.

The next morning, I turn on the news and see continuing live coverage. The father, reporters are saying, isn't talking or cooperating with the police.

I pick up the phone and call my lieutenant. "Has South Pasadena called to ask us to take over the investigation?"

"No," he replies. "They've just called for some advice. Let me call you back."

He does, a few minutes later. "It's official," he says. "They want us to take over the case."

"Let's meet at South Pasadena police department. And let's start from scratch, have them brief us on what happened."

We're told that they got a call about a person passed out in Arroyo Seco Park. When the police arrived, they found a man roughly thirty years old, unconscious, in the parking lot. His clothes were dirty, with dirt caked underneath his fingernails and scratches on the palms of his hand.

The interior and exterior of a BMW were doused with gasoline. In the back, they found a child's car seat.

As the man was transported to a hospital, a woman called the station.

She said her name was Ana Estevez, and she was going through a contentious divorce. Her ex-husband, who had visitation for the week, was supposed to return their son to her at a prearranged location.

"He didn't show," she said, "and he's not returning my phone calls or text messages. His name is Aramazd Andressian. My son is Aramazd Andressian, Jr., but we call him Picqui."

She gave the police her ex-husband's license number. It belongs to the gasoline-soaked BMW that was towed from the park.

A second search of the car reveals prescription pills, two knives, and a child's sweatshirt. It's covered in a film that appears to be vomit.

Andressian, who is thirty-five, is still in the hospital, and no one knows where five-year-old Picqui is. A missing person investigation has been opened.

We take over the investigation. I'm the lead detective. Six other detectives are assigned to assist me. We interview the father.

"I was assaulted in the park," Andressian says. "Somebody must have taken my son."

It's the same story he gave to South Pasadena police.

We interview him for three hours. As Andressian talks, he suggests he's being framed—by his ex-wife. That she arranged a kidnapping to make it look like he had done something to their son.

Not once during our conversation does he ask about his son.

We arrest him on suspicion of child endangerment and child abduction.

"I bet they think of me like some Casey Anthony," Andressian tells a booking officer.

Police and bloodhounds search the park. As my team and I start to go over his phone records, backtracking Andressian's movements and piecing together his whereabouts, we find out that he picked up his son on a Saturday. On Thursday, he took Picqui to Disneyland. We can't confirm his whereabouts after that because Andressian turned off his cell phone.

Andressian, we discover, was spotted by park employees and campers at the Cachuma Lake Recreation Area in Santa Barbara the next day, Friday. K9 units search the area and divers check the shoreline for a body. We check surveillance video cameras in and around the lake.

We come up empty.

Video obtained from Disneyland shows Andressian leaving the park with Picqui at 1 a.m. In the video, Andressian walks about twenty feet in front of his son. They're not holding hands.

One in the morning, with a five-year-old…you would at least want to hold your son's hand or hold him in your arms to walk him back to the car because the kid's got to be exhausted from a full day at Disneyland.

Four days later, we don't have information about where Picqui is, or any evidence. We're unable to press any charges, and Andressian is let go. He tells people that his ex-wife has been following him—and that he's afraid for his life.

Picqui's mom, Ana Estevez, sees us every other day. The woman is an elementary school principal. Picqui is their only child. Before he was born, she had suffered five miscarriages.

Every day she's going places, passing out flyers, trying to get information about Picqui, hoping he's alive.

We search Andressian's home, looking for evidence. We bring in a scent-detection dog. On his computer, we find that Andressian made a new will. He also searched maps of wilderness areas.

The second week of the investigation, Ana Estevez comes to me and says, "What do you think my ex-husband did with my son?"

We have no proof that he killed Picqui. We have no bloody crime scene. We're monitoring Andressian's movements, but so far, we have nothing.

I keep going back to Andressian's body language in the Disneyland security video—the way the father is distancing himself from his son, not holding his hand. It's as though he doesn't want to be physically or emotionally attached to Picqui.

"I think he killed your son," I say gently. "I have no proof of it, and I hope I'm wrong, but I don't think I am."

She breaks down, sobbing.

But she doesn't give up hope. Week after week, Picqui's mom keeps passing out flyers while Andressian is living it up in Las Vegas, partying, doing drugs, meeting up with prostitutes.

It's been two months since his son has disappeared. I find out the father has shaved his beard and dyed his hair—behaviors which are consistent with someone who is going to flee the country.

He's arrested on suspicion of murder in Las Vegas. On a Friday, the day of my daughter's wedding rehearsal dinner, we bring him back to LA. Andressian admits to me that he killed his son up in Santa Barbara, just hours after leaving Disneyland. He discarded the body in an area near Lake Cachuma in Santa Barbara County.

Didn't bury his son, just discarded him.

I get on the phone and coordinate with Santa Barbara county sheriffs to try and find the body. I send detectives and a cadaver dog to help with the search.

My sheriff orders me to go to my daughter's wedding rehearsal. I arrive late to the restaurant. Within a few minutes, I'm back on the phone with my detectives.

They end up recovering the boy's body.

The next day, my daughter gets married. Because I'm still coordinating with my guys up in Santa Barbara, coordinating a next-of-kin notification, trying to get one of my guys to go talk to Ana Estevez, I don't remember a single thing about my daughter's wedding day.

Scene after scene takes a part of you. Homicide after homicide, there's something that's going to stand out to you and stay with you forever.

On January 26, 2020, I'm pulling up to the gym when one of my kids texts me a screenshot from TMZ. It's a breaking story on a helicopter crash in Calabasas involving LA Laker basketball star Kobe Bryant.

A few minutes later, I'm told to head to Calabasas. The

National Transportation Safety Board and the FAA will be handling the investigation. Our department will assist in recovering bodies.

When we arrive at the crash site, we're given manifests of who boarded the helicopter. There are nine people, including the pilot.

There are no survivors.

"I have ten people getting on a plane right now in Washington," an NTSB representative tells me. "They'll be here tomorrow to start combing the wreckage. Can we just hold the crime scene until tomorrow?"

"We can't say we've left bodies on the hillside because your guys are arriving tomorrow—and we need to get to work now. We're going to lose daylight in about two hours."

"Okay," he says. "Just please don't touch the wreckage."

The air heavy with smoke, I'm thinking about Kobe Bryant, the father and husband, a man who spoke Spanish and Italian. I'm thinking about the Chester family, whose daughter and mother were on the helicopter; the Altobelli family; the coach; the pilot who couldn't have woken up that day wanting to die.

In the fading sunlight, I see cell phones lying out and around the wreckage and the remains. Some of the phones are intact. Their screens light up as they ring, family and friends calling, hoping against hope that their loved ones are still alive and coming home.

DREW NICOLETTI

A graduate of the Citadel, Drew Nicoletti served as an Army helicopter pilot and flew medevac missions while deployed overseas. He works as a deputy and pilot for a sheriff's office in Florida.

A carjacking call comes in. The suspect pistol-whipped the driver of a navy-blue Audi sedan and fled the area in the stolen vehicle. Catching a suspect on the run can be difficult, especially in densely populated areas, as the vehicle we're tracking by helicopter generally blends into traffic.

I'm training Steve, who's new to the aviation unit, how to operate the helicopter's camera. As we take off, a deputy is driving directly behind the stolen Audi. We're given his location.

It's a huge win.

I fly while Steve mans the camera.

We locate the Audi in a matter of seconds.

We watch it hit the turnpike northbound. The driver is gunning it, going well over a hundred miles per hour, blowing by every other car, and using the breakdown lane when traffic slows or stops.

I've been a civilian pilot since I was fifteen, and I went to flight school in the Army. After I came back from flying helicopters in Iraq, I found a job flying for law enforcement. It was eye-opening for me, the possibility of assisting everybody and being utilized every single day. Everybody's always asking for a helicopter. It eliminates a lot of things on the ground, a lot of need for multiple officers or deputies. What would take ten people before now takes four guys on the ground and a helicopter, and we get it solved relatively quickly.

We also work really closely with K9, every single day. We're kind of a package deal, K9 guys and helicopter, when it comes to suspect searches. We're kind of the go-to tools to locate suspects.

I go into work every day and I have no idea what I'm going to do that day. I don't even know what airspace we'll fly into, how long we'll be needed, whether we'll need extra equipment. I don't know if we'll be doing high-level surveillance or a suspect chase or looking for a missing two-year-old.

Most of the time, police officers and deputies and federal guys, we're not in this to win some sort of *People* magazine life award. That's not what we're here for. We've all seen basically the worst in people, and we're just going out every day trying to effect a little bit of change. If you can help somebody for whatever reason, and you can try and take somebody who's hurting other people in any way, shape, or form off the street even for a little while, it's worth it.

Not everyone's going to like you, especially when you try and go out and enforce laws. But that is what it is. That's the job. At the end of the day, I think most police officers see the good in what they do.

We wake up every day and we try and do good. We try and do good in our communities and be of service to the people that we serve, and we try to keep good citizens happy and healthy, and we try to take bad citizens away from the good ones so that the good people have an opportunity to prosper and be American.

Most people go out every day who wear a badge and they really try to do the best they can and try to help as many people as possible.

You can't just watch injustice happen in front of you and just turn around and go the other way. It's not how it works. You have to do the best thing that you can for your safety and for the people that you're trying to help.

High-speed chases usually don't end well, and there's always a high risk that one or more innocent bystanders will be seriously hurt or, worse, killed. The cops in pursuit are giving the driver plenty of space. If they get too close, the guy might panic and decide to do something foolish.

I'm flying directly into a rainstorm.

Summertime in South Florida, the horizontal dimensions of a storm can be as much as two miles wide. I've still got to find a way to dodge the winds and rain and still follow the Audi.

I'm doing my calculations when the Audi tears off the

turnpike. It's now heading into a rural area that connects to another county. The deputies there have already been alerted, and they've sent up their own helicopter to follow the vehicles.

My helicopter is a bit more powerful than theirs, but we're both dodging the bad weather.

I get the other pilot on my radio and suggest setting up an altitude separation. "I'm going to go five hundred feet above you. Go five hundred feet below, pick up the Audi, and we'll both follow it."

On the ground, the county deputies need to prevent the driver from negatively impacting any civilians. The Audi is heading north and officers have blocked off the next intersection with what are called Stop Sticks—flat lengths of plastic equipped with hollow, Teflon-tipped steel that pierce, then deflate tires at a controlled rate, designed to prevent blowouts and bad accidents.

I study the road. If the Audi drives over one of those sticks, we'll be able to corral him in a rural area where he won't be able to hurt—

"Shots fired," says a voice on the radio.

Those two words are the most nerve-wracking, adrenaline-spiking, mind-spinning words you can hear as a cop. That's when you lose any idea about what's coming next.

Okay, shots fired. Was it outbound? Who was shooting? Is a police officer the shooter or a target? Who's been hit? The bad guy or a cop—or was it a civilian?

The voice comes back on the radio. "The driver is shooting out the window, at the deputies."

The Audi makes a U-turn, avoiding the Stop Sticks, and

now he's back traveling northbound. A detective is positioned in an unmarked car parked on the opposite side of the road. I watch as it pulls out. A deputy is driving. I have no idea if the move is deliberate, but the Audi drives head-on into the detective's car.

Both vehicles start tumbling and flipping and then come to a complete stop.

The Audi is immobilized. It's not going anywhere.

Deputies and TAC guys in full SWAT gear surround the Audi and take the driver into custody. On my radio, I hear one of the supervisors on the ground place a call for fire and rescue. The deputy behind the wheel of the unmarked car is seriously injured.

We've crossed into the next county, but I've done enough work here to know the locations of its rescue facilities. The closest fire station is a fair drive from here, and even once the deputy is stabilized he'll most likely need to be airlifted to the hospital, which means more waiting. The whole process will take up to half an hour, maybe more.

I speak to Steve over our radio. "Tell the supervisor on the ground that if he needs us to transport the deputy, we can do that."

It's not standard procedure, but we're here right now. We've recently used this helicopter for hoist training and the padded space behind the cockpit is nearly empty. We can load the injured deputy in with our rescue equipment and get him to a hospital in minutes.

Steve contacts the ground commander, who replies, "Yes. Land. Let's do this."

The other helicopter swaps space with me. After it climbs

five hundred feet, to my position, I start my descent. There are power lines right in front of me, so I fly in somewhat perpendicular to the road. I land with the side door facing the group of deputies.

Steve gets out and opens the back door. The injured deputy is receiving first aid. He's suffered a head wound, but he's conscious and alert. In half a minute, Steve loads him into the back of our helicopter.

We're back in the air.

"Where do you guys want us to go?" I ask the deputy on the ground.

"St. Mary's. It's the closest level one trauma hospital."

Flying medevac in the military, I know all about the serious complications high altitudes can cause with head wounds. "We're going to stay below five hundred feet and fly as fast as we can."

Six minutes later, we land on St. Mary's pad. Nursing staff transfer the injured deputy to a gurney.

Twelve hours later, the deputy is released from the hospital.

Catching a carjacker and delivering an injured officer for medical treatment—it's the best six minutes I have as a law enforcement officer.

BRIAN STURGEON

Brian Sturgeon is a full-time police officer and a K9 handler.

I've volunteered to act as a decoy for the K9 unit.

It's four in the afternoon, and I'm sitting in the back of a parked van. It's 110 degrees outside and 130 degrees in the van. On top of that, I'm wearing a fifty-pound bite suit.

No surprise, I'm drenched with sweat.

Training inside a van ratchets up the difficulty level for the dog. A van sits high off the ground. Each dog must jump up and through the driver's-side window and then make its way through an obstacle course of seats.

The next dog comes through the window. He makes his way to me and suddenly he's airborne.

My padded arm is between us. I "catch" him—the phrase K9 handlers use for when the dog bites the decoy's arm.

This is cool. I've been a cop for a few years, have always thought about working in the K9 unit. This experience solidifies my decision. This is the career for me.

K9 units, I learn, work with tactical teams and patrol. They're used as support—to find out where a suspect is hiding, to cover the front or back door of a residence.

Dogs are also used as a show of force. Ninety percent of the time, people don't want to tangle with a dog. A suspect will fight five cops, but when he sees a dog, he'll either decide not to fight or to stop fighting. A suspect will hide from cops but will give himself up once he knows a dog is about to be let off its leash.

A dog's main asset is its nose. A dog's nose is so fine-tuned it can find a gun a suspect discarded while running away from officers. In the US, dogs are bred for looks and docility. That's why we import K9s from Europe, typically German shepherds and Belgian Malinois dog breeds with working pedigrees. After a year of training as a patrol dog, they're usually cross-trained in a specialty such as narcotics or explosives.

My first dog as a handler is a German shepherd. I bring him to a call where cops have lost sight of a suspect. I park about 150 yards away from where everyone has gathered.

One of the officers calls me on my radio. "We saw the suspect down the street," he says. "You're parked too far away."

"Copy that. I just need to give the dog a quick break before we start getting into business."

I bring the dog out to take a whiz. He's sniffing around

when he straightens and whips his head around, looking in the opposite direction from where the officers last saw the suspect.

The dog starts dragging me toward some large bushes.

When you're afraid, your adrenaline is pumping, putting out endorphins that come through your skin as odor. You also release what we call skin rafts, tiny bits of dead and dying cells that continuously fall off your body, creating an invisible (to us) cloud that a dog homes in on.

I get on the radio. "Somebody's right here."

The dog is still pulling. I hold him back and shout toward the bushes, "Come out!"

The dog starts barking. A man stands and surrenders.

Not everyone goes quietly. Some people have a lot to lose if they're caught.

I'm at another scene when the suspect decides to run. If we catch him, he's going to go back to prison.

The suspect's already got a good lead on me, and there's no way I'll be able to make up the distance, especially weighed down by my gear.

A dog can make up the distance, and then some.

I let the dog go. He's a furry heat-seeking missile that runs close to forty miles per hour. He locks on the target and catches the suspect in a full-speed runaway takedown.

It's amazing to watch.

Fourteen years and four dogs later, I'm given a nine-year-old Malinois named Argo. A Malinois is like a German shepherd on crack. There's no chill mode.

Argo and I respond to a domestic violence call in a neighborhood of single-family homes. The caller says his girlfriend is being held against her will by her roommate, a man named George Lee. This district is short-staffed, tied up on other domestic violence calls, so it's just me, Argo, and two other officers.

I meet the officers on a quiet street away from the suspect's residence. It's late morning on a weekday.

"Lee's the homeowner," I'm told. The house is typical of the neighborhood—ranch-style, spaced six to eight feet from the next property, and surrounded by a tall stockade fence.

"He's wanted on two separate open cases, and he's got numerous domestic violence and drug warrants. He's also got a weapons warrant."

They pull up a four-month-old booking photo of Lee, which lists his height as five foot eight and his weight as close to 260 pounds.

This guy's not going to be running or jumping a lot of fences.

The other officers go talk to the boyfriend who called 911. He's in a car parked across the street.

"I'll stay here and watch the back," I say, "in case Lee decides to run."

I stand on the street with Argo, who's on a six-foot leash attached to a pinch collar, and when I look over the six-foot pedestrian gate, into Lee's backyard, I see a male come out the back door.

The man doesn't fit Lee's description. This guy is maybe 150 pounds and doesn't look anything like Lee's picture.

The guy darts around the backyard, looking through the side fence, to the front of the house. We don't have a whole lot of info on who else might be inside the house besides Lee and the female roommate.

I radio the officers. "You've got a male in the backyard, but I don't know if it's the person we're looking for."

The guy runs back inside the house.

A moment later, another male comes out. He's accompanied by two females. They start running erratically around the backyard. The male might be Lee, but if he is, he's lost about eighty pounds in the four months since his booking photo was taken.

The man starts running in my direction. I know he's going to try to escape.

Okay, here we go. I move off to the side. I don't want this guy to see me and then start running another way. We might only have one opportunity to catch him, get it done quickly.

I hear the man come over the fence.

He lands on the ground as I come around the corner.

The man freezes, faces me.

It's George Lee, no question, just thinner. To lose that much weight in four months? There's only one way. Drugs.

"Get down on the ground," I say, wondering if he's under the influence of meth, known as his preferred drug of choice. "Get down on the ground or the police dog will bite you."

Lee turns away from me and scales the neighbor's six-foot fence. I race after him, holding Argo by the leash.

Lee is standing on top of the fence, one hand gripped on the edge of the house roof for balance, and out of my reach. He glances at me over his shoulder but then, instead of jumping onto the other side, he starts to pull himself up onto the roof.

I release Argo.

He scales the fence easily, then jumps another six feet in the air and grabs Lee by the arm.

Lee screams, but Argo won't let go. They fall into the adjacent yard.

I jump up on the fence. I start to go over into the neighbor's patio, and that's when I see a boxer–pit bull mix attacking Argo, who is focused exclusively on the suspect. Lee gets back to his feet and starts to run away, with Argo still biting him, and the other dog biting Argo.

It's a full-on dogfight.

"I have a gun!" Lee shouts. "I have a gun!"

I land on the patio. Lee turns and takes a shooting stance using both hands.

He doesn't have a weapon. His hands are just pressed together, index fingers formed into the shape of a gun.

Sometimes suspects who are under the influence or suicidal decide they'd rather be shot than go back to jail, and will pretend to have a gun or another weapon, hoping to get shot or killed by a cop. Then their family will sue the city and get a payment.

I'm not falling for Lee's suicide-by-cop attempt. "Stop," I say, pulling my weapon. "Get down on the ground."

Lee ignores me and runs to the opposite side of the yard, heading for the fence but still dragging Argo. The Malinois's jaw is clamped down on Lee's arm, trying to pull him to the ground even as the other dog keeps biting Argo.

I holster my weapon and run after Lee. When I get closer, I see Argo has sustained significant cuts on his body. There's a lot of blood.

I jump on the suspect's back. As we struggle, the boxer–

pit-bull-mix dog starts attacking me. Argo won't let go even as I pin Lee to the ground. I grab Lee's left wrist to pull his arm behind his back and cuff him. I glance at his right hand.

He's got a box cutter gripped inside his fist.

I don't have any backup yet. I've got a vicious dog attacking me, Argo is biting the suspect, and the suspect is armed with a box cutter. This thing is unraveling so fast—what do I do? How do I fix this?

If you hit a dog hard enough, it will usually back off and stay away. One hit usually does the trick.

I hit the other dog once. He comes at me again and again. When I hit him a third time, he backs off just enough for me to reach around my waist with my left hand and pull my gun out.

The dog is coming at me again.

I don't want to do this, don't want to shoot someone's dog, but I don't have a choice. I have to protect myself and Argo.

I pull the trigger.

One shot is all it takes.

I reholster my gun. Lee is sweaty and has managed to free his right hand, the one holding the box cutter. He starts to stand, swinging.

I'm within two feet of him yet somehow manage to dodge the blade.

Lee swings again, misses. I need to get some distance from him because now I'm locked in a lethal-force situation.

I back up. Argo manages to keep Lee from advancing.

I grab my weapon and pull the trigger.

My gun malfunctions.

As Lee turns the box cutter on Argo, I perform what's called a tap rack. I tap the floor plate of the magazine, to ensure it's properly inserted and locked into place. I accidentally sweep the ejection port with my pinky finger, causing my weapon to have a "double feed." I now have two rounds inside the chamber where there should only be one.

My weapon locks up. I can't fire the gun until I clear the rounds.

It's a complex malfunction, one that takes time to fix.

As I strip the mag out, Argo knocks Lee to the ground a second time, giving me some much-needed time to fix the problem—and to get some distance away from Lee.

My first assisting unit climbs over the fence and jumps onto the patio. Between the three of us, we quickly get Lee cuffed and searched for additional weapons. Later, I learn that this entire event occurred in only three minutes.

It feels like three hours.

Argo is covered in blood. I scoop him up into my arms, leaving the other officers to deal with Lee, and run Argo to the emergency vet. He's rushed into one of the operating rooms.

This is bad.

The vet calls me at home later that night.

Argo has a puncture to the eye and six cuts—a serious one on his cheek, and a ten-inch-long cut along his abdomen. Fortunately, beneath the fur and skin, dogs have supertough fascia, a network of protein-collagen connective tissues. It protected Argo's muscles, ligaments, and organs from being cut or injured.

"As for his eye," the vet says, "the blade went right between his skull and eyeball. It didn't do any damage. If the blade had moved an eighth of an inch in either direction, he would have lost his eye."

Hearing the news is an enormous relief.

Argo is back to work in ten days.

His work ethic is impeccable. His only goal, ever, is to bring down the bad guy.

If only all our work was so cut-and-dry.

ORLANDO SANCHEZ

Orlando Sanchez works in Special Weapons and Tactics (SWAT).

G rowing up on the West Side of Chicago is all about gangs, guns, and drugs. Every day there are car chases, people are getting shot and stabbed—every bad thing you can think of happens here. Gangbangers dominate the streets of these neighborhoods.

And there's my family. When my old man came back from Vietnam, he tried working regular jobs. One thing led to another, and he got into a life of crime. Now he's incarcerated, and my mom is by herself, left alone to raise me and my three younger brothers.

The gangs jump me all the time, wanting to fight just because it's fun. Once or twice a year, they'll pull out their guns and, laughing, take potshots at me as I take off running.

Seeing and dealing with this shit day after day makes me think this life is normal.

At fourteen, I'm walking to a friend's house when I encounter two gang members. I've decided to fight my way through them when one guy pulls a gun and points it at my head. My hands come up to protect my face. The gun goes off and I take a bullet to the wrist.

I need help, but there's no way I'm going to tell my mom—she'll get hysterical—so I seek out an older cousin. He takes me to the hospital. A doctor removes the .25-caliber round. The wound isn't bad, so they patch me up and send me on my way.

My mother never finds out about the shooting, but she decides to move us to a suburban neighborhood. I'm going to a different high school, but I'm thinking of dropping out so I can help her make ends meet because my father's in prison.

"You're staying here," the school tells me. "You're a bright kid. We're going to work with you, help get you on the right path."

The school puts me into a work program that allows me to make better money for my family. I start thinking about the big picture, the life I want.

I've always been gung-ho about the military and law enforcement, even though I've had negative experiences with cops. In my neighborhood, you can be a good kid, but if the cops come around and see you with a bunch of assholes known for doing bad shit, they're going to treat you like one of the assholes. You're going to get policed.

I'm not mad at the cops. I understand I'm being policed

because of the company I keep. The police are simply doing their job, trying to keep good people safe.

I decide I want to be a cop. To do it, I'm going to need to keep my head on straight, because the second I go down the wrong path, I'm done. Thank God I'm not a follower. I surround myself with better people.

I go to school for automotive repair. I'm nineteen, working in a car shop, when I take the police entrance exam. I end up with a high score. I go through a battery of tests.

It takes three years for Chicago PD to get back to me.

After I graduate from the academy, I'm paired with an older copper who is the father of a girl I knew in school. I'm going to patrol the same neighborhoods where I grew up.

We're driving through the projects when I hear *pop-pop-pop*. Everyone outside is running to take cover as three bullet holes appear on the front hood of the squad car. We have no clue who's shooting at us, so we get out of there as fast as we can.

I do patrols and pull traffic stops and meet people I haven't seen in more than a decade. I get involved in car chases, I run after dudes with guns and rifles—Wild West stuff. Then Chicago PD transfers me from a war zone to a nice neighborhood to do what we call parkers and movers.

This is for the birds, I think, when I'm assigned to write parking tickets for good, hardworking people, citing them for blowing through a stop sign. *This is definitely not for me.*

My old neighborhood is crazy, but I like the action. The suspense. I like being in the shit all the time. There's always something going on. There's never a dull moment.

But the real reason I want to go back has to do with

all those gangbangers and dope dealers who terrorized me as a kid. I despise them and the drug culture. They destroy communities and families—*my* family.

My new partner is Puerto Rican, like me, and also from the West Side. We're aggressive on patrol, looking for dope spots, bangers, and new shooters. We grab the buyers and the dealers. We set up dope deals. The ones who run from us, nine times out of ten it's because they're packing a gun, or they have a warrant out on them. Sometimes both.

My partner and I put away a lot of bad guys. We win the neighborhood back, a block at a time.

Our efforts catch the attention of our bosses, and we're asked to go to the Special Operations Section (SOS), which deals with crime suppression in every district throughout the city. We recover between 150 and 200 weapons every year.

SOS is the place you go when you want to get on the SWAT team. That's where I want to be. I love tactics, fitness. The mindset. All of it.

My partner doesn't make it to SWAT, but while we're together, we do a lot of good policing. The criminals fear us. The neighborhoods are now much safer.

I have no idea the tide is about to turn.

I work full-time for the SWAT team. Our team services the whole city.

Early in my career, we get an email alert about a sheriff who has served a warrant on a guy named Bill Moore, who was involved in a prior domestic incident where he broke his wife's nose. When the sheriff arrives, Moore is holding a handgun. The sheriff bails out and calls the SWAT team.

We set off to the offender's house. A containment team is already on Moore's house. We set up in the guy's detached garage, which is roughly fifteen feet away from the dwelling. The garage offers good cover, and it gives us a direct line of sight to the home's rear door and windows.

A guy inside a BearCat talks over a PA, encouraging Moore to surrender, come out peacefully. Minutes stretch into what feels like hours.

Moore bursts from the rear door. I'm watching him running straight to us.

He's armed.

The garage door is locked, and we've placed ballistic blankets on the windows in case Moore opens fire. He can't get into the garage but knows we're in there; he hears me telling him to drop his weapon and surrender.

Moore won't listen. He's in a rage, screaming at us, well beyond the point of reason. He runs back to his house.

I pull aside a ballistic blanket.

See Moore reexit the door. He runs up the concrete stairs and raises his weapon in our direction.

I open fire and strike him several times in the body. He falls down the steps and then, using a concrete barrier as cover, tries to shoot us. I strike him in his hand. He falls back into his apartment.

He's bleeding out.

We give him verbal commands to crawl out and surrender. Finally, he complies.

I'm involved in a lot more altercations—though I've been

shot at more times as a kid than all my years on the job. And now I find myself in a new world, one where public opinion on cops has turned increasingly negative.

A grandmother runs out of her two-story house and calls 911, saying her grandson has a gun and is threatening to kill her. The police arrive and enter the house, unaware that the suspect is in possession of multiple weapons and ammo.

The shooter, tucked in a strategic location on the second floor, pins down the cops inside the house. The cops don't have ballistic shields to protect themselves—and if they try to flee, the shooter fires at them from an upstairs window, which forces the cops back inside the house.

SWAT is called. I'm one of the first officers to arrive.

I strap an M4 rifle and a beanbag shotgun to my back. Lethal force is only used as a last resort. If we can do something—if, say, a shooter drops a handgun or rifle or pulls out a knife, we'll always go with the less lethal option, provided there's enough distance between us.

I wonder if the shooter has taken someone, maybe another occupant of the house, as a hostage.

In a hostage situation, I'll have two guys with shields flanking my three and nine o'clock. When we breach a door, one guy will go left, the other right, to divide the shooter's attention to, hopefully, allow one of us to take a head shot—but only if we have a clear, clear shot. Our objective is never to hit the hostage.

The rest of the team quickly arrives. I'm what's called the primary operator. The guy who goes in first. I'm also the team leader for my squad, and our shield specialist. I have one shield that weighs twenty-plus pounds and is designed to withstand rounds fired from handguns. The other, heavier shield is used for protection against rifles—and nearly everyone these days seems to have a rifle. People in the streets are getting lit up by rifles left and right.

I grab my ballistic shield. We breach the door, and I move inside, my team funneling in behind me.

Seven cops are pinned down on the first floor. I'm "posted on the stairs"—I stand at the bottom of the stairs, looking up to the second floor, searching for the offender.

I can't see the subject.

"Hurry up and evac these coppers," I tell my guys. "Get them out the back so they're not a liability to us anymore."

We get the cops out safely. The subject, a Black male, stands eight feet away, at the top of the stairs. He refuses to surrender.

Decides he wants to engage me.

There's a huge level of confidence that comes with having ballistic protection in front of me. In a gunfight, the main thing we're always worried about is getting blasted in the face. With a shield, I can hold my position.

The shield comes with a four-by-seven-inch ballistic viewport. I'm pinned down on the bottom of a stairwell, watching the subject as I pull out my Glock 17. I order him to drop his weapon. He refuses to comply. I tell him again, again, and then he raises his weapon at me, intending to shoot.

He's not leaving me a choice. I have to engage.

I whip my pistol around the shield.

Fire five shots in center mass.

I end up killing him.

The blowback is swift. The press sensationalizes the event.

Activists are up in arms. Private citizens take out billboards, saying the shooter was murdered by the racist Chicago Police.

I'm shocked, even though I know I shouldn't be.

I'm a dark-skinned Puerto Rican. I'm from the neighborhood. Most of the men and women I work with come from diverse ethnic backgrounds.

There are a few cops out there who shouldn't be cops. Proactive policing has nothing to do with racial profiling or the color of your skin. It's all culture. Demeanor. The way you act.

Anywhere you go in the city right now, cops have lost control in being able to effectively prevent and deal with crime. They have absolutely zero control. The criminals know this. It emboldens them.

The criminals have the upper hand, they do not fear the police. So that's how it is. That's the truth.

JOHN REILLY

John Reilly's father was a World War II veteran and a firefighter. John worked as a state trooper for over thirty-four years.

It's well after midnight and I've pulled over a speeding car carrying three males. Two are in the front seat, one in the back.

When you're a state cop and working the highway, you're not always dealing with criminals. Speeders aren't criminals, you know what I mean? But these three guys are acting very suspiciously, making furtive movements as I approach. The one in the back is moving around the most.

I'm not a big guy, maybe five seven and 155 pounds. And when it's two o'clock in the morning, and you're pulling over a car with a bunch of people in it, it's dark, you're on the side of the road, you're by yourself—you have to be careful.

The guys are young, in their late teens to early twenties—kids, basically. I have them get out of the car, one at a time, giving very clear instructions about what to do and what not to do. Where to stand.

I've always prided myself in speaking to people of all ages, shapes, and colors with respect. I treat them the way I want my own family members to be treated.

The kid from the backseat starts to walk away from me. His back is toward me. I see him slide his right palm into his belt line, as if he's about to pull out a weapon. He starts to turn toward me.

I pull out my gun, thinking about an incident that occurred on my second day at the academy. Our class was out on a long-distance training run, a cruiser in front of us and an ambulance trailing behind in the event of a medical emergency, when one of my classmates collapsed. They were working on him within seconds and, unfortunately, he still died.

It became a huge story, news articles saying that drill instructors were spitting on him and yelling, "Die, maggot, die."

I was there, and that didn't happen. Right then I learned that I'm going to be at places where things happen and don't get reported correctly.

The honest story is I always wanted to be a firefighter like my dad. The joke always was, he wanted me to be a dentist.

It's the same with me and my kids. I've had an amazing career, I wouldn't change it for the world. But both my sons wanted to go into law enforcement, and I'm afraid for them to follow me into it. The thin blue line, it's not a thin blue line anymore. It's a gray fuzzy area, and it's getting grayer and fuzzier.

I come from all kinds of cops and public servants. What people don't get, in my opinion, is that we're just family guys who want to do the right thing.

"Leave your hands where they are," I tell Backseat Guy. "Do not take your hands out of your pants, or I'm going to shoot you."

"Don't shoot me! Don't shoot me!"

I grab his arm to keep his hand in his pants. I've got to keep my eyes on him while watching the two other guys. If something goes down with Backseat Guy and I get into an altercation, I'm wondering if his two friends will come over and kick the shit out of me.

Or maybe they'll whip out their phones and start recording.

The world is completely upside down.

I unbuckle the guy's pants. I pull them down and see what he's holding.

"You asshole," I say. "You almost got yourself killed and my career ended for a little bag of *weed*?"

"I—I didn't want to get caught with it."

The kid's a nervous wreck.

So am I.

We all kind of hug it out on the side of the road.

BILL McHENRY

Bill McHenry worked in a department of corrections for three years, then became a patrolman in a sheriff's department and, later, a detective, a lieutenant, and the chief of police.

Right before I make detective, I get a strange call. A guy who rented a storage locker paid six months' rent and parked a car in there.

My patrol partner comes by to assist me. We stand outside the unit. The smell is awful.

"You've got a stinker in there," he says.

"What are you talking about?"

The detectives have arrived with a search warrant. I'll work with them on the case.

They open the locker onto a scene out of a horror movie. Thick clouds of flies swarm past us. I cover my mouth and nose against the nauseating smell, but there's no looking away from the sight of a man and woman sitting inside the car, the two bodies in an unspeakable state of deterioration.

The male victim, we discover, is the owner of the car. We also discover that the deceased man's nephew put the car into the locker. The nephew won't talk, but we find out that something went on between him and his uncle regarding the woman, then he decided to kill them both. He put the bodies in the trunk of one car and then transferred the bodies to another vehicle and drove out of state, thinking he would get away with it.

And to a degree, he does. The state prosecutes him, but the double-murder charges fail. The car owner is convicted for concealing a homicide and goes to jail.

Cops decompress by getting together and talking. We have to, because once we go home to our spouses, none but those who also work in law enforcement really understand what we've been through. Explaining our experiences is completely different from living them.

Explaining a case to a suspect nearly throws me.

I arrive at a crime scene, see a guy lying over a deceased woman, hugging her and crying. His name, I'm told, is Louis Sullivan. He's twenty-six, lanky, and has thick red hair.

Officers take Sullivan away for questioning. We need to establish whether he's connected to a number of unsolved rapes of young women. I work the scene, taking notes, documenting evidence, before I return to the station.

"I didn't kill her," Sullivan tells me. "I found her that way."

"You don't know her?"

68

"No, sir."

"Then why were you crying and hugging her?"

"Seeing her like that, it just upset me so much, you know?"

I nod, keep nodding, like I believe him.

"Here's the thing," I say. "That woman had initials carved into her forehead."

"So?"

"The letters *L* and *S*. Those are your initials."

I make an emergency appointment with my dentist, Larry, a former cop.

Larry checks my aching tooth, says it needs filling, then leaves me in the chair.

Suddenly I hear Larry's voice from the reception area. "Okay, okay, don't shoot. Here's my wallet."

I'm a lieutenant, dressed for work in plain clothes. I'm carrying my service weapon.

I'm thinking through my plan when a female dental technician opens the door and, her voice pinched tight with fear, says, "There's a guy out there who's robbing everyone."

Larry is practically yelling to the intruder—"I know you have a gun, but you don't have to put us all in a room and start shooting. Just take our wallets."

I know this is Larry's way of communicating the situation to me.

Then the shooter's voice moves closer to the hall. "Hey, you, the dental tech. Where are you? Are you hiding in that room back there?"

The young woman is hiding behind me. I stick my head out the door.

Lock eyes with the shooter.

He's maybe fifty feet away, and armed. We both fire—*boom, boom,* the gunshots deafening in the small space.

He goes down. I'm still standing.

I quickly move to his body and see that he's taking his last breaths. I grab his weapon, then get close enough to determine if he's still breathing.

He's not. The guy is gone.

I find out later that the shooter had a history of armed robbery. He'd been out of jail for six months. Like other ex-cons, he went back to doing what he knew best—stickups. By some miracle of divine intervention, his street gun jammed when he pulled the trigger.

I thank God daily that everybody inside the dentist's office got out alive.

YORK K

York K is a veteran of the US Marshals Service.

Anthony Blackstone works for the biggest heroin dealer in New York City. Blackstone helps set up the murder of a witness and immediately disappears.

He's been on the run for twenty years.

Blackstone's case file has been handed down almost as a rite of passage. My four predecessors haven't been able to find the guy, and now it's my turn to try and make something happen.

I start with Blackstone's Social Security number. I'm playing around with some derivatives of it and purely by happenstance I get a hit on a man named Dale Bloom. I do some digging into his case and uncover some data that suggests Bloom might, in fact, be Blackstone.

I dig a little deeper, one thing leads to another, and I find out that this Bloom guy has a bank account. I get a subpoena, put everything into motion, and call the bank.

"He's closed the account," the bank tells me. "We're getting ready to send out his check."

"Don't send it. I have another idea."

I'm given Bloom's address. We get the postal inspector to dress up as a legitimate mailman, show him the last known picture we have of Anthony Blackstone. I've already secured the arrest warrant.

The postal inspector knocks on Bloom's door shortly after 10 a.m. while two deputies and I stand off to the side, completely hidden.

The front door cracks open. The postal inspector holds a flat envelope with the actual bank check. It's certified mail—Bloom needs to sign for it—but the postal inspector hands the envelope over without a word. As he turns and walks away, he covertly gives us a thumbs-up.

Dale Bloom is a match for the picture of Anthony Blackstone.

I race up the front steps, past the postal inspector, and knock on the door.

"Excuse me, sir, I forgot to have you sign for your certified mail."

The door cracks open. I rush it with the other deputies.

The little guy standing in the middle of the doorway is dressed in a T-shirt and boxer shorts. He's got skinny legs and arms, but my focus is on his face. There's no question in my mind I'm staring at an older—and balder—version of Anthony Blackstone.

The guy waves his hands in surrender because he knows the jig is up. The deputies secure him.

WALK THE BLUE LINE

"Sir," I say as I cuff him, "please tell me your name."

He glares at me. "You goddamn well know who I am. I'm Anthony Blackstone." He signs, shakes his head. "Twenty years down the drain."

Blackstone is in complete shock. "Haven't seen my wife and kid in over twenty years," he says, more to himself than us. "Two decades and you catch me."

Blackstone is a complete gentleman about the whole thing. Professional. He reminds me of an old Italian mob guy I met briefly not that long ago—a major heavy-hitter, back in the day. I treat everyone with respect, and one day when I'm moving him from his cellblock to the courtroom, we get to talking, and he says, "You know, you guys are making a horrible mistake, all you feds."

"Why's that?"

"You're dismantling the Italian Mafia."

"Meaning?"

"Let me see if I can explain this to you." His tone is very cordial. "These Dominicans you got running around, all that they want to do is to fucking shoot everybody and kill them. They don't care. They shoot their mothers. They shoot their brothers and sisters, even kids. They don't care who they shoot."

He snorts. "Then you got these Jamaicans calling everyone the N-word, and these guys use machine guns, fucking spray and pray. They shoot at you, they don't give a fuck who you are, who they kill."

"So, what's your point?"

"As you're busy dismantling us, these guys that are controlling the streets and neighborhoods are getting more violent.

But here's my point. When the FBI came to arrest me, they knocked on the door. I knew who they was. I says, 'Hold on one minute.' I put on my coat. I grabbed my hat. I opened the door, and I says, 'I'm ready, gentlemen.' It's just business."

Some professional criminals, especially the old-time mob guys, what they do for a living is strictly business. It's nothing personal. They have a certain respect for law enforcement.

That's no longer the case.

Karl Foster's parole requires him to submit to urine tests. His most recent one shows he has "pissed hot"—drugs are found in his system—and now he has failed to report back to his parole officer, a violation which automatically makes Foster a fugitive and bumps him to the attention of the Marshals Service. His case comes across my desk.

Foster is a nobody. His case isn't a big deal—it's a low-level parole violation—but I treat his case as though it is a big deal because I follow a single rule, one I've taught to anyone who works a fugitive case. Regardless of a fugitive's age and crime, if he has a history of violence, I treat each one the same because I never know what I could encounter.

I start working Foster's case and discover he has robbed a couple of banks in Connecticut. The FBI considers him a "person of extreme interest." I manage to get Foster's current cell number.

His voice mail is very interesting.

Foster describes himself as a self-proclaimed revolutionary. A militant. He's antigovernment, antipolice—antieverything. "And no matter what happens," he says, "I'll never be taken alive."

We're tracking his phone signal, gathering resources to find and apprehend him, when his signal dies. We watch for it for days. It never comes back.

It's a minor setback. I've uncovered more information on Foster that shows he's now living in Columbus, Ohio. I call headquarters.

"Foster is a fairly bad guy," I explain. "I'd like to fly out there and conduct my own investigation."

"No. Just send out a lead to Columbus, Ohio."

Meaning, *We have an office in Columbus, Ohio, so why should I pay for your flight, hotel, and everything else when someone in that office can handle it.* The Marshals Service is often frugal, sometimes to the detriment of an investigation.

I send the lead to some guys I know in Ohio and say, very clearly, "Whatever you do, please don't have a handyman go knocking on the door at ten in the morning. This guy is hinky, it's not going to work. Do it a little differently, be a little smarter about it."

The guys from our Ohio office send in a handyman on some ruse. Foster figures it out and bolts. Inside the house, they find a rifle, a couple of pistols, and a silencer, which carries a hefty minimum sentence—and gets the attention of the ATF. They want Foster, we want Foster, and the FBI wants Foster.

Karl Foster has now become a major player.

We upgrade him to a US Marshals Service Major Case.

I'm working a separate case in an area Foster has been known to frequent. The guy I arrest knows Foster—and Foster's new phone number. We get all the appropriate warrants and subpoenas, start tracking his signal, and end up finding what we believe is his new address—a somewhat lengthy process as Foster turns his phone off most of the time, to prevent anyone from tracking the signal.

Foster is still in Columbus, only now he's living in a town house with his girlfriend and another girl. This time I'm invited down to help and I bring with me two guys I work with the most.

We're not sure if Foster is home. We're sitting on his house when we receive some information that he is, in fact, in there. I get this bad feeling in my stomach. My gut instinct tells me I need to be *very* careful with this guy.

If this were New York, I'd gear up with my high-risk entry guys and do a dynamic entry with multiple ballistic shields. Columbus PD, however, has an excellent SWAT team and I decide to use them. While I'm at Columbus PD, coordinating tactical measures, Foster's girlfriend and another female leave the house.

They're followed to a store. The decision is made on the ground to snatch them to question them on Foster's location. This was something I did not want done and said so before departing to brief the Columbus SWAT Team.

It quickly turns to shit.

Foster senses something is wrong—the two women are gone too long, probably—and before SWAT arrives, and because of a series of technical mishaps and Murphy's Law—what can go wrong will go wrong—Foster, holding several large duffel bags, bolts out of the back of the house and into the woods.

My guys and the deputies from Columbus chase after him. Foster drops one of his duffel bags, holding a small cache of weapons, but we can't find him. Drug-sniffing dogs are brought in, helicopters are searching from the sky while our guys and the guys from Columbus PD conduct a massive ground search. It's a huge event.

And a huge failure.

Foster is gone. I'm told to go home and never to return to Columbus, Ohio, again. I look at two deputies I know very well and say, "Do me a favor. Monitor the bus stations. That's how Foster is going to leave town."

Sure enough, shortly after I return home, Foster has purchased a ticket to Atlanta, Georgia—and he has a two-day lead on us. I call our Atlanta office. The marshals manage to track him down to a motel.

"Do you want us to wait for you?" they ask.

It's Friday, the start of the Fourth of July weekend. I have plans with my wife and kids.

The week before I graduated from the United States Marshals Service National Training Academy, we had a speaker, a US Marshals fugitive-hunting legend. This guy shared a story about how he was at his daughter's dance recital when he got intel on a fugitive. He decided to stay at the recital and left the fugitive apprehension to his men.

From his tone and demeanor, I could tell he regretted his decision not to get in on the action. What he said next felt like a prophecy.

"I'm getting ready to retire. Fifteen minutes after I leave, no one is going to remember my name, but I got a wife and kids who know who I am because I made sure they were a priority. I would advise you all to operate your careers in the same manner because I guarantee you, if you make the

Marshals Service your family, you'll end up with no family after you retire."

I take that advice to heart. For better or worse, I make balancing my job and my family the operating principle of my career. I trust the guys in the Atlanta office implicitly and leave Foster's apprehension to them.

The marshals do a dynamic entry. Foster reaches into a bag holding a Ruger Mini-14, a lightweight semiautomatic rifle, and a fully loaded AK-47 assault rifle. He's taken down before he can get his hands on a weapon.

"That's not all," one of the Atlanta marshals tells me over the phone. "The town house back in Columbus? Foster told us he knew y'all were watching and coming for him. Son of a bitch was sitting on the upstairs bed with stacks of magazines and—get this—he'd placed a mirror in the hallways, so he could see y'all coming. He had every intention of killing each and every one of you, go down in a hail of bullets."

Thank God we didn't end up rushing the house. If we did, we would have all been in a world of hurt.

The FBI field office in New York City needs help finding a fugitive named Razi, a young male gang member with multiple arrests. He's now wanted for murder. Razi pulled his car up to a rival gang member, pulled out his gun, and shot the guy. Then, for the coup de grâce, Razi got out of his car and pumped several rounds into the guy's head. Razi drove away with his hand out the car window, two fingers held up in a V for victory.

Fugitive investigations require a certain nuance and skill set. I search through Razi's arrest record, paying close attention to people he called. I'm hunting for an anomaly—a one-off phone call, someone he may have called after he got arrested. Someone who may have been overlooked by cops and the FBI.

I find a phone number Razi only called once. The number, I discover, is no longer in service. We finally track down the person who owned the number. It belongs to a woman who now lives in the projects with her young daughter.

For twelve days, we've done research and looked at the case from every possible angle. The Bureau hasn't spoken to this woman—no one has.

Is she a friend of Razi's? A past or current girlfriend?

I look at Nick, a big Greek kid, and TJ, the new kids we've got working with us, and say, "You know what? Let's swing by and get a look at this place. I want to get a feel for it."

We drive to the projects. The elevator for the building is out, so we take the stairs to the eleventh floor. It's coming up on 3 p.m.

We move to the front door of the apartment. Behind the door, in the background and very faint, I hear a noise, like a TV or radio.

That doesn't make sense. If the woman and her daughter are home, why is the TV or radio or whatever's playing turned down so low in the middle of the afternoon?

Nick and TJ stay near the apartment while I go two doors down and knock on a neighbor's door. An old man answers. I ID myself.

"Can you tell me who lives in that apartment?" I ask, pointing.

"A woman lives there with her daughter, but she don't

get back till five thirty at night. She picks her daughter up at school."

The old man is very nice, tells us all sorts of things about his neighbor and her daughter—especially how the woman and her daughter stick to the same schedule during the school week. How the daughter is never left home alone. He tells me he saw the two of them leave this morning.

I move back to the apartment. I can still hear the faint sound in the background.

I knock.

That faint sound disappears, as though someone shut off a TV or a radio. Now, it's silent.

There's somebody in there.

I hear scurrying inside the apartment. I get on the radio.

Can't get through because I'm stuck in a dead zone.

I turn to Nick and TJ. "Whoever is in there, the only way he can escape is through this door. The doorway is a fatal funnel, so stay to the left and right of it in case whoever's in there has a weapon and decides to start shooting. Stay against the walls—they're made of cinder blocks, the rounds can't penetrate—and do not go anywhere near the peephole. I'm going to run downstairs so I can get a signal and call the cavalry."

I reach the stairwell, check for a signal. Nothing, just as I suspected. I race all the way downstairs, step outside the building, get on the radio, and call for the cavalry. I make my way back up to the fourteenth floor.

I'm somewhere on the eighth, maybe tenth floor, when I hear screaming above me.

I rush back up. Nick and TJ have a guy pinned on the floor and lying facedown just inside of the apartment doorway.

"Secure him," I say to TJ. Then, to Nick: "Help me clear the rooms."

I step over the guy, don't even bother to look at him, too focused on making sure no one else is hiding in the apartment.

It's empty.

The apartment has a landline. I call the office.

"Cavalry's not needed," I say. "We're inside the apartment."

"Is it him?"

"I need to check. I'll call you back in a few minutes."

Nick and I grab the cuffed guy and stand him up.

"TJ and I were standing off to the left and right side," Nick explains to me. "Door opens, and this guy here sticks his head out and looks right at me. At that point, I was committed. I bum-rushed him and knocked him down."

I look to our suspect. "What's your name?"

"Virgil Tibbs."

It's the name of the fictional Black homicide detective who works with a white Southern police chief in the movie and TV series *In the Heat of the Night*.

"Does this look like the set of *In the Heat of the Night*, you asshole?"

He starts crying and gives us his real name. Razi, this guy who executed a gangbanger and drove away holding up a hand in V for victory, is crying like a little girl because the Marshals Service is here, and we've got him.

DANNY BROWN

Captain Danny Brown works for a sheriff's office in the South.

Part of my work as a military policeman is to protect and defend the army base at Fort Jackson 24/7. I'm parked in a construction zone on a main roadway on the base when a civilian truck races by at two in the morning.

According to my radar, the driver is going thirteen miles over the speed limit. That's not a huge amount, but it's enough for me to decide to pull the truck over, since it's late at night and I want to make sure the driver isn't impaired in any way.

The man behind the wheel is dressed in civilian clothes. I don't recognize him—Fort Jackson is a massive base—and he doesn't say anything when I ask for his ID.

In the MP world, you can write two tickets. The first one

is a DD Form 1805. It's a money ticket. The fine is low, but it goes on your record.

A 1408 is a warning ticket. It doesn't go into your record, but it does go to the company commander. Warnings, from my point of view, go a long way in reinforcing the importance of safety rules, so I decide to write the driver a 1408.

There's a spot on the ticket where you put down the offender's rank and unit. I check the driver's ID. His rank says "07."

This guy is a one-star general.

I'm a Pfc—private first class, the third-lowest rank in the Army. My primary job is to carry out orders by commanding officers. And here I am writing a ticket *to a general.*

I decide to treat him as I would anyone else, hold him to the same set of rules. I walk back up to the truck and salute him.

"I didn't recognize you, sir," I say. Then I hand him the ticket. "Sir, that ticket is going back to the highest command in your unit, which is, well, you. So, when you get back tomorrow, you're going to explain to yourself why you were speeding."

He laughs. "You sure I was speeding?"

"Yes, sir."

"You were sitting in that construction zone, right?"

"Yes, sir."

His stare lingers on me for a moment. *Is he testing me? Expecting me to say I made a mistake?*

"Yeah," he says, "I was flying, coming through there. I really appreciate what you do. Thanks for keeping us safe out here."

I get back to barracks at 6 a.m. for our shift change. Two hours later, there's a knock at my door. Two day-shift MPs, dressed in full uniform, enter my room.

"Colonel needs you in his office right now," one of them says.

The colonel is a provost marshal. In civilian terms, he's the police chief of the base.

"I'll be up there in a minute."

"You're coming with us right now."

Damnit. He's going to chew my ass out for giving a ticket to a general. It happens all the time—someone of higher rank trying to intimidate, talk down, or lay into me for doing my job.

I follow the men to the military police station. The colonel is seated behind his desk. I salute him and then stand at attention.

"Did you pull over a one-star last night?" he asks.

"Yes, sir, I did."

He gives me a look that practically screams *What the hell were you thinking?*

"General sent this for you," he says, and hands me a military coin. It has the general's name and rank. It's a coin of appreciation.

"He said you did an outstanding job keeping us safe last night," the colonel says.

When I leave the Army and become a civilian police officer, I quickly discover that the mentality I used as an MP doesn't translate well to civilian life. In the military, I was taught to be assertive. Short and sweet. In the civilian world, it comes across as rude.

Also, in my new role I don't have a squad or a team with me or directly behind me. I'm riding solo, as happens in a lot of rural or neighborhood jurisdictions. One thing I learn, fairly quickly, is not to get myself into situations where I'll have to fight.

I'm working the south end of our county when a call comes over the radio about a suspicious person involved in what appears to be a drug deal taking place behind a convenience store. Dispatch gives the address and a physical description of the suspicious person.

I'm half a block away, so I drive over through the woods and pull up along the side of the store. I get out of my car, and when I turn the corner, I see a guy that fits the physical description hand off something to a woman. She walks away.

The guy's back is to me as I approach.

My radio chirps.

The guy turns around, sees me, and takes off running. I chase after him, across the parking lot and then into the middle of the road. He bolts across the street, and when I catch up to him, we're in someone's backyard.

He stops running. High fences surround us. He's cornered.

The guy takes up a fighting stance.

"I'm not fighting you," I say.

I pull out my Taser gun, give him another warning. He ignores it and comes after me. I pull the trigger.

The Taser probes are attached to wires. They release from my weapon and hit him. Instead of collapsing, he does a spin move that looks straight out of a Michael Jackson video—then throws his arm around the Taser wires and, with a swift, hard pull, yanks them from my gun, severing the electrical connection.

He takes off running. As I chase after him, I insert a fresh Taser cartridge.

He hops over three fences before I manage to tackle him.

When it comes to physical altercations, I can't be afraid. I've got to protect myself. I've gotten my ass handed to me several times, but when I'm in the middle of it, I rely on my training, give it everything I've got.

We start fighting in a front yard. In the chaos, I notice a telecom bucket truck parked across the street. The truck's extendable hydraulic boom is raised, and I can see someone standing in the bucket, working on the cable lines.

I manage to get on top of the offender. I pull out my Taser. I need to incapacitate him long enough so that I can cuff him.

He manages to yank the Taser from me. Now we're locked into what's considered a deadly force encounter.

I see a blur of movement from the corner of my eye. Someone bumps me, trying to push me off the guy. I lean to my left, catch sight of the end of a flathead screwdriver fly past my head.

Someone's trying to stab me.

I think of the lineman I saw standing in the bucket. *Why would he come down and attack a police officer? That doesn't make any sense.*

Eight, maybe ten guys are coming from across the road. They're carrying metal poles, bricks, and pieces of concrete—and heading my way. I can tell, by the expression on their faces, that they're not coming to help me.

The person with the screwdriver stabs me in the thigh once, twice. I don't even feel it, I'm so jacked up on adrenaline.

Someone starts yelling at my attacker and the approaching mob to back off. It's the civilian lineman. I didn't see him get off his bucket. Now he's putting himself between me and the advancing crowd.

The guy with the screwdriver is still going after me. I disengage from the fight and back up into the yard, gaining enough distance to safely draw my weapon.

My suspect runs away. The man with the screwdriver stands frozen.

I hear approaching sirens. They're growing louder. *The lineman must have called 911.*

We end up arresting twelve people.

I find out that the house where the suspect and I were fighting belongs to his grandmother. She saw us from across the street, where she was at a gathering with other family members—the mob who came to the suspect's rescue. The man who attacked me with the screwdriver is the suspect's father.

K9 units are quickly dispatched. The dogs locate my suspect, and we get him into custody.

When my adrenaline recedes, I discover I was stabbed six times with the screwdriver. No gaping wounds, just flathead-sized pokes across my right leg.

The father tried to stab me in the head. I could have easily been killed by him or my suspect or by one of his family members. But someone was looking out for me that day: God, or my guardian angel, or a civilian lineman brave enough to put his own life at risk to save a police officer.

On my way to the station, I keep thinking about that mob. In the aftermath of 9/11, the public looked to nurses, medics, cops, and soldiers as heroes.

These days, it's hard for people to trust a blue uniform. But the backs of our cars, shirts, and bulletproof vests say DEPUTY SHERIFF PEACE OFFICER. That's our job. To keep the peace.

JENNIFER FULFORD

Jennifer Fulford works patrol in Florida.

ispatch receives a call from an eight-year-old boy. The cell phone he's using keeps cutting in and out. There are strange men in his house, he says, but he doesn't know how or why.

I'm a field training officer, working the day shift. My trainee and I get called to back up two deputies working the boy's neighborhood.

I'm two months shy of my third anniversary with the department. I ask my trainee why he decided to repeat his training after he'd made his way up to sergeant with a small municipal agency.

"The other place I worked was too slow," he explains. "I want more excitement."

I'm very conscious that promotions never come easily to women. It's assumed that men are competent, that they'll meet expectations required to advance in rank. Only when a woman proves she's competent will she be awarded the same respect.

When I arrive at the small beige ranch home trimmed in white, deputies are already on the scene. No one debriefs me about what's happening. Later, I'll find out that after deputies pulled up, they found a male loading green duffel bags into a red Isuzu SUV parked in the driveway. The male saw them and then casually walked back into the house.

A woman stands in the driveway. I go over to her, my attention on the attached two-car garage. The right bay door is open. I can see the rear part of a gold vehicle that is either an SUV or a minivan.

The woman is the homeowner. She confirms that there are three men inside her house, but she doesn't know what they want, or why they're here. Her kids are in the minivan parked inside the garage. She points to the gold vehicle, then stops talking.

I know there's more to the story—there always is.

Officers who answer a call are considered the primary unit, so they take lead. I'm waiting for the deputy to make an action plan, but he's already moved off to examine the backyard. My trainee is standing on the street, watching the other side of the house.

I stare at the minivan, gripped with an overwhelming feeling. We need to get the kids out of the vehicle *now*. I turn to the deputy and say, "I'm going into the garage."

I remove my sidearm, a Glock 21 that fires .45-caliber rounds. As I move up the driveway, I can see two doors inside the garage. One leads to a laundry room. The other, painted a dark red, opens into the house. That door is directly opposite the front of the minivan.

I step inside the garage and see a Toyota SUV, parked and empty of passengers. I turn to the minivan. In the back third row, two very small kids are buckled into their seats.

I don't see any sign of the eight-year-old boy who made the 911 call.

I try the car door handle.

The minivan is locked.

I hear raised voices.

I move to the rear of the minivan and look to a deputy, who is standing in the middle of the driveway. "There's an argument happening inside, and it's escalating," I say. "There are two kids locked inside the minivan. We need—"

Four gunshots sound.

As soon as I crouch down behind the wheel well of the minivan, the dark red door opens and this huge guy rushes into the garage. He's standing near the front of the minivan, eight, maybe nine feet away—shooting at me.

I'm using a car full of kids as cover.

I come up and fire.

A round hits him in the pelvic area.

In TV shows, the guy who's shot flies across the room. Reality is nothing like that. When I hit the shooter, his body slumps as if sitting down into a chair. He's still conscious—and he's still shooting at me.

I jump back behind the minivan and start looking around

for escape routes. That's when I notice movement up in front of the van and see *another* shooter.

He must have snuck out behind the first guy.

The three of us exchange gunfire.

When I'm empty, I do a quick reload. The first guy I hit is up and shooting his weapon. I fire and hit him center mass. He slumps over and drops his gun with a groan. Right then I know he's no longer going to be a problem.

But I have a problem: he shot me in my right shoulder. I look down and see my Glock lying on the garage floor. I'm telling my arm to move but it's as if my nerves have been severed. I can't move it—and now the second guy is leaning across the hood, firing his weapon at me.

Suddenly I'm thinking about my friends and family, all the stuff I still want to do with my life. My mind quickly cycles through the stages typically associated with grief—first anger, then acceptance. I'm determined to win, not to let him kill me.

First, I need to stay in the gunfight. I've recently completed a training on offhanded shooting, the technique to use if your strong hand's injured. The instructors taught us at how to draw and reload a weapon. I pick up the gun with my left hand.

We exchange more rounds. One of mine hits him in the head. He disappears behind the van and doesn't come back up again.

The woman said there were three men. Where's the third guy? Where's the eight-year-old boy who called 911?

I examine myself, surprised to see that I've been hit not once but multiple times. I'm bleeding from several gunshot wounds. Other than the shot to the shoulder, I had no idea I'd been hit.

Seeing the blood, I start to feel light-headed.

Breathe. You have to stay conscious. Breathe. There's a third guy gunning for these kids—and you have to protect them.

One of the deputies and my trainee pull me out of the garage and bring me to the front yard. The deputy is screaming at the dispatcher, "Officer down, we need help!"

The fire department can't come to an active shooting scene, so I'm carried by several people to the fire station at the end of the block.

Later, I find out that SWAT had been called. People were evacuated from the surrounding homes. When I listen back to the radio traffic, I discover I was inside the garage for fifty-one seconds.

To me, it seemed like forever.

The third shooter, I learn, surrendered to one of the deputies. SWAT then moved into the garage and removed the children from the minivan.

The eight-year-old was inside with his siblings. I didn't see him because he was hiding under a seat. The Department of Children and Families has been notified.

The mother, I find out, tried to flee the scene on foot, without even knowing if her kids were okay or not. She and her husband had 300 pounds of pot and $60,000 in cash inside the house. That morning, after the mom had loaded her kids in the minivan, to take them to school, the Isuzu SUV parked in front of the minivan, to prevent it from leaving. Three guys got out. The husband, they knew, was out of town, and they had come to collect the drugs and the money.

The Department of Children and Families return the kids to their mom.

I've been shot ten times. Seven directly hit my body. And the other three: one hit my Taser, the other my shoulder mike, and the third one went through part of my uniform.

I have nerve damage in my arm, and surgeons had to reconstruct one of my ankles.

The media is hounding the department for information. Two weeks after the shooting, I take part in a press conference. A reporter asks me, "Don't you feel bad? You took a human life."

"It wasn't my choice," I reply. "I just reacted to what they did."

My dad comes to me and says, "What are you going to do now?"

"I'm going back to work."

"Why on earth would you want to do that?"

Because I want to help people. I want to solve crimes, get involved in what's going on in the world. We're not going to catch every bad guy, but it's important for people to know they can feel safe, that there are people out there fighting to protect them.

MATT BURROUGHS

Matt Burroughs works as a patrolman in the Southwest.

You want to be a cop?

The text is from my buddy Steve, who owns the Cross-Fit gym where I work out. He's a sheriff's deputy and has been on the job for twenty-plus years. I'm twenty-seven and have recently finished a seven-year stint in the military.

I reply, Sounds interesting.

You should apply.

Okay. Send me the paperwork. I'll do it over the next couple of days.

No, no, no. You have to apply tonight.

By what time?

In the next two hours.

I've never given any thought to being a cop. Right now, I'm

working odd jobs here and there. I decide to apply, see what happens.

My application is approved. I go through the rest of the process, pass the mandatory polygraph test and all the physical and mental exams. Next stop is the police academy.

I want to do this.

My academy class is going to be the last one that goes through the old paramilitary-style training. Still, the goal is to achieve competency in the new style of detail-driven police work based on college-based learning, computer skills, and teamwork.

That's where my military service gives me an edge. I understand the process, the method behind the madness of a drill instructor getting in your face.

I'm surrounded by twenty- and twenty-one-year-olds who have never been yelled at, never been screamed at, never been told what to do. They've never pressed their clothes, let alone a uniform. I show them how to use an iron to press military creases into the sleeves, back, and body of their uniform shirts, so they don't get their asses chewed out every day.

The number one rule I was taught growing up is that complacency will kill you. That rule was reinforced in the military and now, again, by the police academy. Being on top of your stuff—fitness, practicing, and keeping up with tactics and case law, knowing what's happening in the news—is the key to success no matter what uniform you wear. Complacency is what gets you hurt or killed.

The academy, like basic training, can try to create educational scenarios, but it can't prepare you for dealing with the unpredictable reactions of real people to real situations.

When my field training officer (FTO) pulls up in his car, I've got all my stuff, my gun, vest, and radio. I climb into the passenger seat and right off the bat, we get a call about a traffic accident.

Okay. No big deal.

"Did you read the call text?" my FTO asks.

The screen says the accident involves a head-on collision on a two-lane road. Multiple witnesses report the driver of the car going sixty miles per hour was ejected through the front window.

My FTO starts driving nearly twice that speed, lights on and sirens blaring. To reach the scene, we're ducking and dodging cars tangled in rush-hour traffic. All my senses are heightened. My heart's pumping and my hands are shaking.

Oh, my God, this is intense.

As an academy trainee and now as a rookie on the job, I've tried to absorb one all-important lesson. *Know where you are at all times—especially when you're alone.* You can't always rely on GPS.

If I'm sitting alone in my squad car and someone starts shooting at me, if I don't know where I am, I can radio for help, but my colleagues won't know where to find me. As we get closer to the scene of the accident, I start committing street names and other details to memory.

We're the first ones to reach the ejected driver. He's lying on the ground, bleeding out from a head-trauma wound.

"Okay," my FTO says, pointing at the driver, "let's get to work."

I throw on my gloves. I have training in first aid and advanced trauma, and when I start bandaging up the driver's head, I know he's going to die, I know I'm watching him die.

I check the driver of the other car, check him for bleeding and injuries, while radioing traffic officers to roadblock the area, prevent oncoming cars from smashing into us.

People who witnessed the collision have parked their cars around the site. "We saw what happened," some of them call out, while others are standing on the side of the road and glaring at me like *Hey, you're here to help, so help.* I've got to make sure they don't leave so I can get their stories. We'll need them for the investigation.

I'm experiencing the biggest adrenaline dump of my life.

My FTO and I finish up, and when we hop back into the car, we're called to a Walmart parking lot.

I've gone from dealing with a fatality to a woman panicking about having some stuff stolen from her car. *I just watched someone die on the side of the road and now you think your car getting broken into is a big deal? You have no idea.* But at the same time, you got to have empathy toward them.

"I'm so sorry this happened to you," I tell her.

The adrenaline is still dumping into my system, I'm still focused on my last call.

From there we're called to a trailer park. A woman resident is experiencing a psychotic episode. Social workers won't show up if there's a weapon involved, or if someone can't—or won't—cooperate. When that happens, they call us.

The woman is covered in urine. She's screaming and kicking, won't let us anywhere near her.

"Okay," my FTO says, "put handcuffs on her."

Handcuffing people is hard. It's even harder when your hands are shaking. My adrenaline has fired up again, and my hands are shuddering so badly the handcuffs are rattling. I go to cuff her and keep missing her wrists. She keeps fighting me off and my FTO is evaluating my every move.

Oh, my God, this is harder than I thought.

Finally, I get her cuffed. I'm going to need more practice.

When I get back to the station, my hands are still shaking so badly I can't write the case report. I take in a bunch of deep breaths.

This is going to be my life every single day. There will never be a steady pace.

After two weeks of training with my FTO, I'm off on my own. I receive a call from dispatch about a possible domestic violence incident at a local park. The girl who calls 911 says, "He's trying to beat me up. I'm running into the desert, I'm leaving. Get here right now. I need help."

When I arrive, nothing is going on, and there's no sign of this girl who called 911. I question the people at the park, and they all tell me they didn't see this girl or any incident, everything's fine.

I'm about to drive away when a young guy approaches my vehicle.

"I know you guys are getting a bad rap with everything that's going on," he tells me, "but I just wanted to say thank you for what you do. A lot of people in this community—in this state—appreciate what you guys do every day to keep us safe."

"Thank you. I appreciate it."

Before the girl hung up, she told the 911 operator that her male attacker drives an old white Ford Bronco that has a temporary tag on the back. That's it, that's all I've got for information.

I drive up a dirt road. I take a right and see a white Ford Bronco pass me on the southbound lane.

I turn around and follow. I get right behind the Bronco.

It has a temporary tag. This might be the car.

I hit the sirens and lights and glance at my small computer screen. The map is dotted with the current GPS locations of a couple nearby squad cars.

As the Bronco pulls to the side of the road and parks, I call dispatch and give the location where I may have spotted the vehicle involved in the possible domestic violence call.

The driver gets out of the Bronco.

I'm already out of mine, walking straight to him. "Get back in your vehicle," I tell the driver.

"My girlfriend has heart problems." He's Latino, in his mid- to late twenties and roughly six feet. "She's in the passenger seat."

Another deputy pulls up.

"Okay," I tell the driver. Then I turn to the deputy. "Stand with him. I'm going to check on the girlfriend."

As I approach the vehicle, I can see her inside. She appears to be half asleep, but I see that her eyes are black and blue and that she's bleeding from a broken nose and split lips.

I unclip the radio from my vest. "I need medics and an ambulance. I have a victim with possible head trauma, I don't know what from."

At the sound of my voice, she stirs and widens her swollen

eyes. She looks at me with what I can only describe as sheer terror. I've never seen someone so scared.

Then she sees that I'm a cop and says, "Please help me."

"I've got you, you're safe. I'm not going to leave your side until the medics arrive."

I keep talking to her as I take close-up pictures of her face and wounds. She tells me her boyfriend has prior domestic violence charges. When she ran away from him, he caught up to her and dragged her into the SUV.

Smashed her face repeatedly against the dashboard.

She was in so much pain he made her drink from a bottle of vodka. Then he gave her a pill to quiet her down.

When the medics arrive, I immediately go up to the boyfriend and put him in handcuffs. I begin to read him his rights.

"Sir," he says. "Sir, can you hear my side of the story?"

I deployed a few times when I was in the military. I've seen the worst people can do. Those experiences helped me prepare for this job, but right now I'm seething with so much anger I can barely speak.

"Yeah, absolutely, man, I *absolutely* want to hear your side of the story. What happened?"

"Well, sir, she tripped and fell."

Hearing his blatant lie takes my anger to a level I've never experienced. It's the first time I truly understand the expression "seeing red."

"You know what?" I say, escorting him to the squad car. "I appreciate your side of the story, sir. Thank you. But due to facts and circumstances, you're still being arrested for domestic violence."

"All of you cops are the same. You guys just want to fucking arrest a Mexican."

I don't say anything. I don't speak to him during the ride to the jail. I just take his ass in there.

People say, "It's your duty to protect and serve," but that isn't true. It's my duty to enforce the law. That's how I protect and serve.

They can defund us all they want, but the truth is, this is a calling. I took a pay cut to join the police department because it's not about the money. Honestly, I enjoy going to work. I hate to even miss a day. I just really like going and helping people.

LEON LOTT

Leon Lott is the sheriff of Richland County, South Carolina. In 2010, he traveled to Iraq to help set up the Iraqi government's first all-female police academy. In 2021, Lott received the National Sheriff of the Year award from the National Sheriffs' Association.

On a typical boring Saturday night during the summer I'm sixteen, my friends and I decide it would be fun to egg some cars.

I'm a baseball player, with a good arm. I'm able to hit a lot of cars.

Especially police cars.

We get caught and arrested. My hometown is small. Everybody knows everybody.

One of the cars I egged belongs to Officer Patrick Stone.

He lives in my neighborhood. When my dad works evening shifts, he can't take me to church on Sunday, so Officer Stone picks me up and brings me to church with his family.

Stone looks at me and says, "You know, you could have killed someone."

"There's no way I'm going to kill someone by hitting a car with an egg."

"Really? What if your grandfather had been behind the wheel?"

Stone knows my grandfather, knows he's elderly and frail with a heart condition.

"If your grandfather was driving and you hit his windshield," Stone says, "he might've run off the road and hit a tree. He could've died. Did you ever stop and think about that?"

I didn't, but I'm thinking about it now. It never occurred to me that throwing a few eggs, something I viewed as harmless and fun, could have such a disastrous consequence.

It really opens my eyes.

Not only am I arrested, as part of my punishment I'm also going to end up going through a mandatory diversionary program where, Officer Stone tells me, I'm going to be washing a lot of police cars and doing a lot of wind sprints and other military-style physical activities. As bad as it is getting arrested, what's even worse is that now I've got to go home and tell my parents and my grandmother, who is visiting from Chicago, what I did.

The idea of disappointing them fills me with fear.

Attitudes today are completely different.

There's a lack of respect for authority, a lack of respect for life, and a lack of role models. When I grew up, parents disciplined their kids. Today, parents say, "My child doesn't do anything wrong. My child is perfect, so it must be your fault." It feels like the blame is always being redirected onto someone else.

And the violence... violent crime is rising, and the criminals are getting younger and younger. When I started out as a cop, people got into fights. Now, instead of throwing eggs, they're throwing bullets.

Improvements have to happen on both sides. I start with my side.

When I become police chief in a small town called St. Matthews, I go to my first community meeting and ask the crowd what they think of their police officers.

An older lady says, "We call y'all cops without legs."

"What do you mean by that?"

"We ain't never seen none of y'all get out of a car. We don't know if you got legs or not."

She's right. Our officers don't interact with the community. I want the community to not only respect our officers but to also appreciate what we do.

We start putting officers into schools to work with kids. We start a program called Project Hope, which ends up helping reduce crime against senior citizens. We start doing crime watches in neighborhoods and in business sections.

When my officers have free time, I tell them to get out of their cars and build relationships. They've got walkie-talkies. If they're needed, we can get in touch with them. So if I see an officer sitting on a porch and drinking a glass of iced tea and talking to people, I don't think they're goofing off. They're doing exactly what I want them to do.

Later, when I'm elected sheriff of Richland County, South Carolina, I bring these programs with me. Except now, instead of my four officers in St. Matthews, I have nine hundred people—so we can do these programs on a much larger scale.

The concept shouldn't be cops versus the community. It should be the community and cops working together. That's what community-oriented policing is—cops and the community working together with the goal of preventing crime. And if we can't prevent crime and something happens, we work together to solve it.

We've got bad cops. We've got bad soldiers, bad priests—every profession has someone bad in there. But it's law enforcement's responsibility to make sure we're not all seen that way, and we do that by building relationships with the people we're serving. We need to build a solid foundation so that if—or when—there's a critical episode, the community will stand together. You can't build a relationship with anyone during a crisis.

People want to be heard. Our job in law enforcement is to give them opportunities to be heard. And to listen.

If you want to become a cop, be one who makes a difference. Change the narrative. Be part of that change and make a difference in people's lives, every single day.

PART TWO:

Serve

LAURA McCORD

Laura McCord works for a police department in the South.

"My momma just got shot."

The person on the other end of the line is a twelve-year-old male named Trevor.

"She's lying, like, facedown on the bathroom floor," Trevor tells the dispatcher. It's coming up on midnight. "There's a lot of blood, but I think she's fine. I heard her breathing."

"Did you see who shot her?" the dispatcher asks.

"No."

"Was this a break-in?"

"I think maybe my stepdad did it."

"What's his name?"

"Marty. He drives a blue truck."

The dispatcher tells him to hide under his bed. That's the

last thing I'm told as I set off with my partner and a couple of squad cars.

It's January, and I live in a state where we really don't get snow. It happens to be snowing tonight, making the highway slick. Trevor's address is in the southern part of the county. Now I'm trying to drive our Crown Vic across uphill gravel roads without getting stuck. The last road is so steep I decide not to risk it. We park, get out, and walk. As I climb a hill, my focus is on Trevor.

When I was in high school, I was a victim of a violent crime—one I didn't report until years later, when I was nineteen. That was when I was introduced to how the criminal justice system works.

A female investigator was assigned to my case. The way she handled it and how she treated me changed my life, to the point where I said to myself, *This is what I'm going to do for a career.* I signed up for criminal justice courses at a technical college and declared my major. The rest, as they say, is history.

Trevor lives in a small ranch home the size of a cabin. An ambulance arrives as a couple of the officers veer off to search the property for the suspect. My partner and I enter through the home's front door.

A woman with blond, curly hair is lying facedown in a pool of blood. Just as Trevor described, she's in a hallway near a bathroom.

A door to a bedroom is shut. We search the rest of the house. The suspect isn't here. EMS enters, gets to work.

There's no question in my mind this woman is dead.

I think back to what Trevor told the dispatcher—*I think she's fine. I heard her breathing*—and I realize what Trevor heard was the sound of his mother drowning in her own blood.

I find Trevor standing in his room. He's in shock. I identify myself, tell him he's safe.

It's cold, so I grab some of his outdoor clothes. Then, using my body as a shield so he doesn't have to see his mother's bloody body again, I navigate him out of the house.

Victims have a range of responses to trauma. People might say, "Well, the victim wasn't crying, so he must not have been sad," misinterpreting the symptoms of shock.

That's the case with Trevor. He's not crying. He doesn't seem scared. His expression isn't blank but more along the lines of *What just happened?* As we drive to the Crimes Against Children unit, I ask him if he's hungry.

"We can stop at McDonald's," I say.

Trevor doesn't answer.

I try to engage him in conversation, asking him if he likes sports. He opens up a bit, tells me he likes football. His favorite team is Clemson.

The investigator assigned to Trevor's case happens to be my very first field training officer. Sheila is also the sergeant for the Crimes Against Children unit. She knows I want to work with young kids and juveniles. I ask her if I can sit in on the interview.

"Sure," she says. "You've built a rapport with him."

I take a seat next to Trevor. He's looking at a small stuffed purple gorilla on the sergeant's desk.

"Would you like it?" I ask him. "The toys here are for brave kids like you."

"No," he says, "I'm good."

Sheila asks Trevor what happened at his house.

Trevor is in his bedroom when he hears arguing. He leaves his room and sees his stepfather sitting on top of his mother and physically assaulting her. Trevor isn't a big kid, but he manages to push his stepfather off his mother.

The mother and stepfather continue arguing. Trevor goes back to his room. He lies down, and as he's dozing off, he hears a loud bang.

"It shook the entire house," Trevor says. He's very soft-spoken. "Then I smelled lead."

He runs out of the bedroom and finds his mother.

His family doesn't have a landline, just a cell phone. Trevor sees his mother's iPhone, covered in blood, on the sink in the small half bathroom. He steps over his mother's body, grabs the phone, wipes away the blood from the screen, and calls 911.

Sheila gets a text. She stands and signals me to join her outside her office.

She closes the door. "The mother didn't make it."

I knew the mother was dead. Now it's our job to tell Trevor.

We head back inside the office.

"Trevor," Sheila says, "I'm sorry to tell you this, but your mommy didn't make it."

"What?" Trevor stares a moment, then shakes his head. "No, she was breathing, I heard her breathing."

I move closer to Trevor. "Are you sure you don't want that little stuffed gorilla? He's purple, we can name him Clemson."

"I can have him?"

"Absolutely." I give it to him.

Trevor holds the stuffed animal. He starts rocking back and forth. Tears are rolling down his face, but he doesn't make a sound.

The night of the shooting, Trevor's stepdad, Marty, drives into the next county over and goes to a store to buy more beer. Afterward, he spots a police checkpoint. Marty thinks the police are out looking for him (our officers are actually stopping and searching vehicles for a missing elderly male). Marty turns around and drives back into the county where he lives.

Using pieces of mail from the house, we're able to track down Marty's full legal name, his date of birth, and the truck registered in his name. We send the details out over the radio.

That night, two cops see the blue truck, pull it over, and detain Marty for further questions. A few hours later, Marty is charged with murder, possession of a weapon during the commission of a violent crime, and unlawful conduct toward a child.

The stepfather refuses to admit he shot Trevor's mother.

Suggests that Trevor, this quiet, good kid who is involved in Boy Scouts, committed the murder.

Marty sticks to that story even after we find enough evidence to bring him to trial. Trevor is the key witness and, unfortunately, is forced to testify.

Trevor does an amazing job on the stand. The stepfather is sentenced to life without parole for the murder, plus fifteen years for other charges.

*   *   *

I go to work for the Crimes Against Children unit. I'm assigned a case where a mother is so high on meth and other drugs that she leaves a trash bag in her four-month-old's Pack 'n Play. The filthy house is filled with addicts doing drugs and having sex. The little boy suffocates to death.

I attend the autopsy. I stare at the chubby infant, wanting to revive him. What sticks with me, though, are my interactions with the parents—how little they care about their kid's death.

I can't stop thinking about Trevor, who is now living with his grandparents.

After the autopsy, I text my husband. I'm having a bad day.

Want to go home and have a drink? he replies.

No, I don't. I don't want drinking to become a habit. I don't want to use alcohol to help me forget.

I reach out to a friend.

"You're doing God's work," she tells me. "You're protecting these children."

I've developed a ritual where every evening after work I set aside half an hour, sit in silence, and get lost in a good book and a cup of coffee. Even during these quiet moments, I'm thinking about Trevor, wondering how he's doing.

I need to move on from that case, but I don't know how.

My mom comes up with an idea. "That bracelet you wear, the one with all of those little charms?"

"My Pandora bracelet." It marks significant events in my life.

My mom says, "Why don't you get one in memory of Trevor and his mother?"

I go to a jewelry store and in a sea of charms I find a little baby gorilla.

"That's it," I tell the saleswoman. "That's the one."

PAT WELSH

Pat Welsh was twenty-eight years old, a practicing assistant district attorney and married with two kids, when he decided to give it up to pursue his dream to become a police officer.

It's two o'clock in the morning and I've been dispatched to a residence in Dayton, Ohio, involving a missing twelve-year-old named Junior.

The address is in a low-income neighborhood where families, predominantly headed by single mothers, live in less-than-ideal conditions.

When I pull up to the house, I see that the owners clearly take pride in their home. Green grass covers the front yard, and all the bushes are neatly trimmed.

I knock on the door. A mom and dad answer. They invite

me inside. Every piece of furniture and decor is immaculate and squared away. We stand in the foyer and talk.

"Our son has been running with the wrong crowd," the mom says. "We're not on welfare, we both work, but we can't afford to get out of this neighborhood because we're sending him to a private school. He's running with the wrong boys in the neighborhood and didn't come home from school today, so we reported him missing."

"Do you have any idea where he might be?" I ask.

"He came home about half an hour ago."

"Is he hurt, anything like that?"

"No, no. He's fine."

"He's literally right here in the house?"

They both nod.

"Okay," I say, "I'll cancel the broadcast. But if he does this again, be sure and call us, and we'll come back and take a report." I'm anxious to get back to my cruiser and do some "real police work," when the mom says, "Will you talk to him?"

The dad says, "We're at the end of our rope. We don't know what else to do."

"Sure," I say, because it feels right. "But let me talk to him by myself. I don't want you guys in the room."

They have a little sitting room and bring me there. Then they bring Junior in and introduce him. The kid says nothing, just plops down in a chair and hangs his head.

I'm a thirty-something skinny white cop. What can I possibly say to a young Black man that will make a difference?

For the next ten minutes, I talk to him as if he's one of my own kids. I'm sure I'm not saying anything his parents haven't already told him, but I keep talking on the chance that he's listening.

The entire time, Junior just stares at the ground. Not once does he ever speak or make eye contact.

I get up and leave, thinking, *I'll probably be back, the kid really doesn't stand a chance in a neighborhood like this.* It would be a while, but I learned I was totally wrong.

Years later, James, my former partner who is now a sergeant, calls and asks me to help him at a scene involving a twenty-eight-year-old Black man who is experiencing some sort of mental breakdown. His mother has been recently widowed, and now her son is refusing to leave the house and get into the waiting ambulance.

I enter the house.

The first thing I notice is a damaged wall. Chunks of plaster and plaster dust line the floor near the wall that is full of holes and cracks. The door on that wall leads into a bedroom.

Thump and tiny chunks of plaster fall from the wall.

I approach the door.

Thump.

I move around the corner.

I ask Sarge how I can help.

"We're going to send you into the room first," Sarge explains. Two other officers are with him. "You're going to dive on top of him."

The other two officers are as big as James—and James is a badass, knows how to handle himself. He's also a black belt in the martial arts.

I look in the room, about to ask the obvious question, when I see this guy and he is a twin to Mike Tyson. Sarge tells me, "There's not a lot of space in the bedroom, and you're the smallest guy on duty. Once you dive on him, then we can move and assist."

"Can I at least try to talk to him first?" I ask.

"We tried that already, but sure, go ahead."

I enter the room, keeping my distance from mini-Mike.

Thump and tiny chunks of plaster fall from the wall.

Thump.

One of the biggest men I've ever seen is sitting on the floor, rocking back and forth. He slams his back and the back of his head against the wall—*thump*—and mumbles, "Oh, God, oh, God, oh, God." It's winter, the window is open, and he's not wearing a shirt, shoes, or socks, just shorts.

He doesn't make eye contact with me. He appears catatonic.

I squat down and introduce myself, "Hey, I'm Pat, what's your name?" Nada but rocking and *thump.*

I have an idea. I duck out and move to the living room, where his mother is sitting.

"Your son," I say. "Is he religious?"

"His father was a pastor. My boy has been like this ever since he died."

"What's his name?"

"Christopher."

I go back to the bedroom.

"Christopher," I say. "Who do you pray with?"

He stops rocking and looks at me. "Nobody," he says.

I tell him, "If I agree to pray with you, will you get up, get dressed, and let me take you to the hospital?"

He nods, yes. He gets up, gets dressed, and I walk him

out. No handcuffs, no ambulance ride, just me and him go to my cruiser.

I pray with him in the cruiser and then drive him to get the help that he needs.

As a Dayton police officer, I'm required to live in the city—a policy known as mandatory residency. At the time, Dayton is the seventh-most-violent city per capita in the United States.

When I'm off duty, I carry a gun in an ankle holster. It's with me as I stand in line, behind a little old lady, at a Kroger supermarket. I don't make eye contact with anyone. I just want to get my groceries and get out of there.

The girl behind the counter is ringing up my groceries when a voice to my left says, "Hey, Welsh. Is that you?"

When people call you by your last name, it's either a cop or someone you've arrested. I turn my head and see a six-foot-two Black male in his early thirties.

He's not a cop—he's not anyone I know.

Is this someone I arrested? Did I send him to prison? Is he out for revenge?

"You probably don't remember me," he says.

"No, sir. I don't. May I ask who you are?"

"When I was twelve years old, you came to my house because I ran away."

I vividly remember the call—my only conversation with a runaway juvenile. He never spoke that day, but now he tells me what he's done with his life.

"I graduated from college," he says. "I'm married and have two daughters. I just wanted to say thank you."

Here I am, being a hard-ass cop, putting up my self-defenses and going on high alert, and it's all because someone wanted to thank me for having an impact on their life eighteen years earlier.

My words back then *did* make a difference.

When I travel the country speaking to other cops, I stress the importance of always coming from a positive mindset. Keep thinking, *This could be a great opportunity to do something good,* and you may have a positive impact on someone's life—even if you never hear about it.

BILL EVANS

Bill Evans is a veteran of the Cook County Sheriff's Police Department.

I n Cook County, police officer training starts in one of two places: the court system or the county jail. It's my choice where to build the practical, real-world experience I'll draw on when I become a cop.

I go to work in the maximum-security division at the Cook County Jail, the largest single-site jail facility in the world. The place is famous for notorious inmates such as Al Capone, the Prohibition-era crime boss of the Chicago Outfit, and John Wayne Gacy, the serial killer whose sinister alter ego was Pogo the Clown.

My first day as a correctional officer, I feel an adrenalized mixture of awe and nerves. Here I am, a twenty-three-year-old kid from a decent Irish Catholic community on the south-west side of Chicago, walking into a jail that houses twelve thousand inmates and takes up four city blocks.

I've volunteered to work in the Abnormal Behavior Observation (ABO) unit, the toughest part of the jail, where the worst criminals in Cook County are housed.

Every day, I go on shift with two other officers. We're locked inside the ABO unit, face-to-face with a dozen of Chicago's most notorious criminals. Although I'm confident, even a little bit cocky, in my physical abilities as an avid boxer, I realize that here I'm dealing with dangerous men who lie more often than they tell the truth.

ABO inmates are constantly, successfully reading us—even as we're trying to read them. They are patient and tactical, always probing for weaknesses while plotting to gain any advantage: extra time on the phone, maybe an extra tray of food at dinner.

They have an uncanny ability, almost a sixth sense, to pick up personal details—like where I grew up, people I know from my neighborhood—or recognizing when I'm tired or I've had an argument with someone or I'm having a bad day.

At the end of every eight-hour shift, I leave exhausted, as though I've given blood. Working in that atmosphere, my senses constantly heightened—it's draining to the bone. I'm also going to school nights, working on a second college degree.

This assignment is temporary, I keep reminding myself. *Stay alert—and keep learning. What you deal with in the ABO, what you see, it's all going to help you as a police officer in the streets.*

Now's the time to pay attention to what I call little keys.

In the ABO dayroom, I find plastic chairs stacked in front of the TV. Atop the makeshift throne sits a gang leader wearing a crown from Burger King. He may be dressed in a bed-sheet cape and cardboard crown, but this guy is conducting serious business. He's asserting his jailhouse leadership while running his gang on the outside.

When things get real quiet in the dayroom—when two inmates start walking a little bit slower or if someone reaches down to tie their shoes—that's a "little key," a signal that something bad is about to go down.

It's a forty-minute drive from Cook County Jail to Ford Heights, named after the stamping company that Ford Motor Company operates there.

The community of fewer than five thousand people struggles economically—to the point that it was once rated the poorest suburb in the US—and the area doesn't have a functioning police department. I'm working as a watch lieutenant under a system where the sheriff is responsible for patrolling the town. Given the limited number of patrol cars, we get a little extra help from the gang crimes unit.

Park Avenue is a very hot block for shots fired calls. Every night during the summer we're getting calls about "shots fired" or "man down." We always respond with two or three patrol cars, and every time we arrive the shooter is gone.

The theory is the gangs are playing us. Either they're setting up to ambush us when we arrive or, equally possible, they're trying to keep us focused on Park Avenue and away from whatever business—moving weapons or dope—they're doing on the other side of town.

As watch commander, I prefer to be out on the streets with my team. Having an extra body can only help, Plus, I want to make sure everyone gets home safe.

One early-autumn night, I'm working with an excellent patrol officer named Karen. We get a shots fired call and arrive on the block thirty seconds later, just as another squad car arrives.

I put two guys on the sidewalks. Karen and I walk down the middle of the street. Our weapons are drawn. We're going to canvass the area to see if we can come up with a shooter or a weapon.

The air reeks of gunpowder. There are barely any working streetlights, so nearly everything appears dark. The entire area is still. Quiet.

Suddenly, I sense "little keys" all around me.

The intuition I developed at the jail is in overdrive, pumping adrenaline and giving me this intense feeling that something awful is about to happen. That we all need to leave *right now*.

I turn to Karen for a gut check. "Is it me, or is this really, really eerie?"

"I feel like they're watching us."

That intense feeling of danger grows stronger with each step.

I give the order to move out.

I'm on patrol with my partner when a call comes over the statewide radio. Four bad guys fled a crime scene in a stolen car. They've passed Chicago city limits—and Chicago PD jurisdiction. Now Illinois State Police are in pursuit on I-55, with a helicopter following in the air.

I recognize the voice of the state trooper providing the details. He's a good friend of mine.

My trooper friend is coming down Cicero Ave. My partner and I happen to be in the area, so we decide to set up on the intersection, try to prevent any vehicles from coming through and potentially crashing.

The searchlight flashes from the belly of the helicopter. It shines down on the highway, moving fast in my direction from about a mile away.

The bad guys and the state police vehicle pass us without incident. No one gets hurt.

My trooper friend, I notice, is driving the only vehicle still in pursuit. I decide to assist. I radio my sergeant about what my partner and I are doing.

"Terminate the pursuit," he says. "Let the state police handle it."

"Sarge, the trooper is by himself. He's pursuing a car with four bad guys in it."

"Okay, continue on. I don't want you to leave him by himself."

The bad guys obviously know where they're going. They're driving fast and reckless through side streets, hoping to shake us off—or possibly leading us into a trap.

The stolen car turns and flies down an alley.

The trooper flies down the alley.

My partner and I follow. It's like a chase scene out of *Starsky & Hutch*—we're bouncing up and down in our car and knocking over garbage cans, anything that's in our path, sending objects flying into the air.

When we shoot out of the alley, I see that the stolen car has come to a full stop. The bad guys are bailing out of it. One guy is so fast, he disappears in the blink of an eye.

My trooper friend was a college running back who played with the Green Bay Packers for a short time. He tackles the driver within fifty yards. My partner goes after the third guy, and I take the fourth.

My suspect runs past a fence and then ducks into a back-yard. I reach the fence a few seconds later. I take out my weapon, turn the corner for a quick peek, and "cut the pie"—visually slicing the backyard into sections.

I spot the suspect twenty yards away.

As he starts running, he turns and fires straight at me.

I see the muzzle flash, hear the *pop* of the gunshot as I drop my flashlight.

I get on the radio. "Shots fired. Suspect just took a shot at me."

I pick up my flashlight and run around to the other side of the yard to confront the suspect, knowing that I'm putting myself in a position where I may be forced to discharge my weapon.

I've been a part of seven police shootings—I didn't pull the trigger on all of them, but I was there, involved in some capacity as a witness or supervisor—and every time, the officer who pulls the trigger is devastated.

I don't want to be put in that position again.

I want everyone, including the suspect, to make it out of this alive. I want to do my job and go home.

I reach the other side of the yard.

Find a cop standing there.

There's no sign of the suspect.

Nearly fifty police officers converge on my location. They interpreted my radio report of shots fired to mean an officer had been hit.

Helicopters search from the air as we scour garages, abandoned homes, parked cars, checking everywhere we see. We spend a long time that night looking for the shooter.

We never find him.

To this day, I keep thinking about how close that shooter was when he fired. To this day, I still don't know how he missed me.

NICOLE POWELL

Nicole Powell, a 2015 National Institute of Justice (NIJ) Law Enforcement Advancing Data and Science (LEADS) Scholar and a 2017 International Association of Chiefs of Police IACP 40 under 40 Award winner, works for the New Orleans Police Department.

I was born in Mississippi and grew up tough and tenacious from playing sports with the country boys. Sometimes, as a police officer, I still have to fight.

My first assignment is working the Eighth District, the French Quarter in New Orleans. Cops here typically deal with tourists and people who've gotten intoxicated on Bourbon Street, where drinking happens twenty-four hours a day, seven days a week.

When I get a call about a disturbance at one of the local

restaurants—a drunk male who's knocking on people's doors and getting loud and unruly—I get the suspect's description and start to canvass the area.

I find him running down a street.

I can't wait for a male officer to come and back me up. I get out of my patrol car and pursue the suspect on foot.

The man is six five. I'm five four. As I gain on him and bear-hug him from behind, attempting to wrestle him to the ground so I can cuff him, we get into a tussle. He manages to get a hand free, lands a couple of punches. Then he changes tactics, starts making a series of jabbing motions over his shoulder. I refuse to let go and push him to the ground.

A male citizen rushes over and intervenes. "You don't hit a woman," he says to the suspect, helping me pin the man down. "That's something you don't do."

I manage to handcuff the suspect before my backup arrives.

Soon thereafter, I find out that the suspect had a knife but dropped it during our struggle. That jabbing motion he made over his shoulder—if I were taller, he would have stabbed me in the head. I never saw the knife because I was too busy trying to hold on to him.

The event triggers a memory from when I was in academy. A field training officer was killed in the line of duty while responding to an armed robbery in progress.

An academy staff member addresses us. "This is the reality of being a police officer. No officer wants to get into a fight, to get shot at or to shoot anyone. But always keep your mind sharp for what-if scenarios. When they happen, be prepared to make split-second decisions. Remember, there's no such thing as a routine call. Every situation you deal with could be a matter of life and death."

The news of the field officer's death causes a moment of self-reflection.

Is this job what I really want to do?

"If you want to serve your community, if you want to make a difference regardless of the possible obstacles you may face, then this job is for you," the staff member says. "If it's not, you might want to consider another line of work."

My thoughts turn to Lieutenant Ben McNair, an officer I met when I was working as a dispatcher for the Hattiesburg Police Department, where only two women are employed as officers. They're not in a supervisory or leadership position.

"You know," McNair says to me one day, "you'd make a great police officer."

I hadn't been thinking about a career in policing. My original goal was to become a doctor, but I decided to drop out of college.

"The Hattiesburg Police Department could use someone like you," he says. "You should think about it."

I have no interest in policing, don't give it a second thought.

McNair is heavily involved in the community. He has a medical emergency and passes away while playing in a youth basketball game.

Even after McNair is gone, his words stick with me. Resonate. Kindle an inner fire to become a police officer. A woman in a supervisory or leadership position. I go right into the police academy.

* * *

Most new police officers are quickly drawn to a specialty—traffic, narcotics, undercover, the detectives' bureau or investigative unit—but that doesn't happen to me. Instead, I learn an unforgettable lesson: being a female police officer in New Orleans is tough. I came from a small town, and now I'm working in a big city.

For those not in the "clique" of the important and influential, getting certain assignments is difficult. I apply for several positions, but never get accepted.

It's frustrating. I feel stuck. I want to do more. Do better. I want to elevate myself in my career. No one gives me any guidance, and there aren't any female mentors.

When a new policy comes in from headquarters and I don't understand all the specifics, I ask my sergeant for clarification.

"Shut up and do it," he says.

Then I get a new sergeant. His name is Cyril Davillier. He makes me print out my reports and edits them with a red pen. He hands my reports back to me covered with red lines and marks.

At first, I think he's doing this to punish me. Then I realize he's doing it because he wants me to be a better writer and investigator.

He encourages me to go back to school. "Education is important," he says. "It will help you expand upon what you're already doing in policing. And it will get you promoted."

The New Orleans Police Department and the National Institute of Justice have a deal with a local community college. I attend, graduate with my associate's degree. Then

I go to Loyola University New Orleans. I'm going to get my bachelor's degree and then pursue my master's.

I'm still working patrol when I get a call about an attempted suicide—a disabled young man confined to a motorized wheelchair.

Being a police officer isn't restricted to saving someone from physical injuries. Sometimes it's about sitting down with people who desperately need to talk—and need someone to really listen. People, I'm learning, want you to hear *their* voice, *their* perspective.

This is my first interaction with a person openly talking about killing himself.

"I don't want to live no more," he tells me. "I'm tired of living in the condition I'm in, tired of not having any help and of people making fun of me. I just want it all to end. I just want to die."

We sit and talk.

"Can you buy me something to eat?" he asks.

There's a Popeyes Chicken not too far away. I buy him lunch, and we talk some more.

"You have a lot to live for," I tell him near the end of our conversation. "And how you're feeling...there are other people in your situation who feel the same way. You could talk with them, share your experiences. It might help you with what you're going through. And it might help them, too."

I tell him we'll get him some assistance—and we do. I continue to check in with him. Our intervention changes his perspective on interacting with the police. It helps him view us as people whose job, at the end of the day, is to help people.

A few months later, the suicidal man leaves a note for me at the police station.

I really wanted to die. But talking to you saved my life. Thank you.

I want to become the kind of officer who builds the kind of trust and legitimacy that humanizes the police. I want to help build services and programs that reach people in need, when they're at their worst.

I'm not the only officer seeking out positive interactions with the public. NOPD has created a peer intervention program called Ethical Policing Is Courageous (EPIC). It empowers officers to police one another, to intervene before a wrongful action occurs. EPIC is a radical cultural shift.

I've been on the job for three years when Hurricane Katrina hits New Orleans. The police department, the city and state—we're all unprepared for its devastation. The hurricane is massive. Our infrastructure, including power and water, fails. Homes and neighborhoods are destroyed. Thousands of people are homeless.

We mount search and rescue operations, using Army cargo trucks called a deuce and a half. The truck is a beast; it can handle almost any type of terrain—except where the water is so deep we need to use boats.

Dead bodies are everywhere we look. Floating in water. On the ground and stuck in buildings. Communications are down, and the only thing we can do is tag the bodies and give their locations to the people who are going around picking them up.

I've never felt so helpless in my entire life.

Two police officers commit suicide. A lot of officers have simply up and left: some because they can't psychologically handle what they're seeing, others because they need to help their families evacuate. We're understaffed. The National Guard comes in to assist with rescue operations and help us maintain law and order.

Close to downtown, I find a woman and her kids stuck in a hotel. As I wade through fast-moving water full of debris to reach them, I see that the woman is holding a newborn who can't be more than a month old.

"Take my baby," she says.

"No, miss. You need to come with your children."

She glares at the waist-deep water, panicked.

"I can't swim."

"It's okay," I say. "We're here to help you."

I've been a cop now for nineteen years. I received a master's degree in criminal justice from Loyola University. I'm also an adjunct instructor there and teach in the Department of Criminology and Justice.

Times are changing. The world is changing.

Law enforcement is also changing.

The media doesn't promote the good things we do within our communities. And there are good things happening every day across the nation, whether we realize it or not. We're in the business of saving lives and building true relationships within our communities. Sometimes it's just sitting down with someone and having a conversation. Sometimes an ordinary citizen decides to intervene and help.

We're human. We need to share these stories.

Our stories.

BOB LINDEN

Bob Linden is a veteran of the New Jersey State Police.

It's 2 a.m. when my trooper coach and I pull into the small parking lot that separates our state police station from a privately owned automobile repair shop.

I'm new to the job and still developing my observation skills—watching everything and knowing what's around me at any given moment.

In the dark, I see a guy climbing out a ground-floor shop window. He's easy to spot because his sweatshirt and sweatpants are bright orange.

I turn to my trooper coach and, pointing, say, "That doesn't look right."

He laughs. "Yeah, that's not right."

We drive over, park the car, and approach the man.

He sees us and tries to crawl back through the window.

We stop him. He doesn't put up a fight.

After some back-and-forth, he finally admits to breaking into the repair shop, hoping to find some money and some stuff he can sell.

My trooper coach shakes his head. "Did you realize the state police station is right next door?"

"Oh, yeah," the guy replies. "I figured you guys would be out on patrol or something."

I'm parked in the back of the station setting up my car to go out on daytime patrol. It's a blazingly hot and humid July day.

I'm signing on with dispatch when someone knocks on the rear passenger-side window. The sound startles me a bit. I turn and see a young guy in his twenties.

"My friend is deep in labor," he says. "There's no way we can make it to the hospital in time."

I step out of my car and see a Plymouth Neon parked a few feet away. It's a small car, not a lot of room to maneuver.

"Okay," I say, more calmly than I feel. "I'm going into the station. I'll be right back, but I want you to move her into the backseat of your car—and crank up the air conditioning."

We call for an ambulance. In the meantime, I gather two of the troopers: one is a former nurse, and the other trooper's mother was an OB/GYN nurse, and she'd given him a "birthing kit." They both come out with me, and as they open up the kit and get to work, I talk to the woman in the backseat. It happens that my wife is pregnant with our first child, so I've been going through childbirth classes with her, learning about the importance of breathing.

In our hot parking lot, I hold the mother-to-be's hand, coaching her through breathing exercises. She's doing well, but a part of me is nervous. Even giving birth to a child in a hospital can be risky. Out here in a car? Anything can happen.

Please, God. Please let this woman and her baby make it through this.

We help the mom give birth to a healthy baby boy. We have him all swaddled up before the ambulance arrives.

The driver I've pulled over for speeding on the New Jersey Turnpike hands me a New Jersey license. His name is Jason Greene, and he's driving a Ford pickup. He's a stocky, muscular guy in his early thirties—and he's clearly angry at being pulled over but is keeping it in check.

Because of the turnpike's proximity to Newark International Airport, we get drivers from multiple states and countries. This guy's license is local, but there's something wrong with it. I just can't put my finger on it.

Teenagers buy fake IDs to purchase alcohol and to get into nightclubs. An adult male only carries a counterfeit ID when he wants to hide his real identity from authorities.

I call dispatch and hand over the driver's info, to see if Greene has any outstanding tickets or warrants. But I want dispatch to expand their search, check if the name Jason Greene is listed on any additional databases. I ask dispatch to dig a little deeper.

Then I wait.

Minutes tick by.

This is taking too long. I want to keep the driver as calm as possible. I exit my vehicle and make up some excuse that we're having problems with the computer.

"Okay," the driver says. "No problem."

I get back to my car. Wait.

Dispatch finally comes back saying that the name Jason Greene was found on the National Crime Information Center (NCIC), a database that contains information on criminal records, missing persons, fugitives, and other criminal information. It's a known alias for a man named William Elliot, who is wanted for murder.

I want backup. I see which patrol cars are nearby and contact the closest one.

I exit my vehicle and walk to the truck's driver-side door. I'm on high alert now, thinking through the many things that could happen. My focus is locked on doing my job and doing it properly.

I knock on the truck window.

He rolls it down.

I keep my voice calm and casual. "Unfortunately, we're still having a problem with the computer. It should only be a few more minutes. Until then, I need you to take the keys out of the ignition—"

"Why? What for?"

I don't want him to take off. I need to get him out of the car, need to tell him something believable, so I focus on "driver safety."

"See all these cars rushing past us? I don't want one of them to hit you. The longer we're here, the more the risk increases, so I've got to ask you to follow procedure and give me your keys."

"All due respect," he says, an edge creeping into his voice, "you're delaying me. I've got a business to run, and I need to get home, like, *now*. So, how about you just write me a ticket and I can be on my way?"

I'm nodding in understanding. *His flight sense is building. He's trying to talk his way out of this. If I don't get his keys, he could drive off. I don't want this to turn into a car chase.*

"I can't write a ticket until I get confirmation from dispatch," I say. "It should only be a few minutes, and then you'll be on your way, I promise."

He thinks it over for a moment.

Removes the key from the ignition.

"Can you hand the keys to me, please?" I say.

He does. Now I've got to get him out of the pickup so that when backup arrives I can arrest him.

I walk around the front of his truck, so I can keep an eye on him, and open the passenger-side door. I peek inside, looking at his hands, the seat and floor.

I don't see a weapon.

"Let's go stand at the back of the truck," I say. "We can talk there one-on-one, and not have to shout over the traffic."

He furrows his brow in thought, then sighs and climbs out of his truck.

I put my hand on the small of his back as I escort him along the shoulder and off to the side, away from the rush of traffic.

The guy's muscles are hard. Rigid. They're tensing to fight or to run.

Another troop car—lights flashing but no sirens—pulls onto the shoulder and parks behind me. My guy glances over at the trooper who steps out. My backup walks casually in our direction. When my backup gets closer, I say, "Turn around, you're under arrest."

My cuffs are already out. Before he can reply, I have him cuffed.

He starts telling me I've made a mistake, but he doesn't resist.

I say a prayer to God, thanking Him for getting me through another day.

The next day, I get a call from a detective in Newark. He thanks me for finding Elliot.

"Great job picking up on that phony license," he tells me. "We've been looking for this guy for years. Now we're going to be able to put him away for a long, long time."

HANA BATIT

Hana Batit grew up in the Middle East. She works on the West Coast.

I joined the Army at eighteen.

In my country, the military and police work together. From the time I was a kid I always knew I wanted to be a police officer so, after basic training, the military pays me to attend the police academy.

Putting on my police uniform for the first time is an incredibly emotional moment—and I've been assigned to the same station where my grandfather, who was also a police officer, once worked. I'm following in his footsteps.

Trainees are immediately thrown into the deep end of the pool. I respond to riots and terrorist attacks. I work with a lot of victims of sexual assault. Helping victims who are unable to help themselves gives me a sense of pride and accomplishment—and purpose.

Then I meet a man from America. We fall in love, get married, and move all over the world before settling in California. I learn English and, because of my accent, I have to speak slowly so people will understand me. I go to college and become a US citizen. My husband and I start a family.

But I'm incredibly homesick.

The United States is *huge.* My country is smaller than New Jersey—and American culture is completely different.

I also feel like I have no direction. And I miss being a police officer.

I share my feelings with a friend, who is a police officer for the sheriff's office. The following day, he takes me to his station and gives me a tour.

"You should come work here," he says. "It might remind you of home."

I sign up. Now I must attend the American police academy.

For the most part, the training is the same. Women in America are treated much better than in Israel. Middle Eastern Arab males mostly ignore female cops, even when you tell them they're under arrest. Their attitude is, "A woman isn't going to tell me what to do." American men aren't surprised when a female cop stops them.

Other than that, nothing I learn comes as much of a surprise. American violence mirrors that of my home country. And the laws here, much like where I was born, seem to favor criminals and not victims. Criminals get released very quickly.

I'm sent to work in the county jail system. After eight months, I'm transferred to patrol training for nine months.

Here is where I find the biggest differences. It's eye-opening.

What shocks me the most is the number of citizens who own guns. Where I grew up, ordinary people are not allowed to own weapons. Terrorists and bad guys are armed with bombs and knives. In America, everyone seems to have easy access to guns. People carry weapons with them all the time, even when they're driving.

I respond to a call where an armed man is trying to hang himself. I arrive, along with multiple units. We draw our weapons, and as we make our approach, I see a man standing on an elevated platform, a rope tied around his neck, a pistol held by his side. Right now, the barrel of his handgun is pointed down, at his sneakers.

But that could change in a split second. He's extremely upset. Despondent.

Fortunately, he tosses the gun in the nearby bushes. Then it hits me: I recognize him. He's a homeless man who lives on the streets with his girlfriend.

The homeless issue here in California, I've discovered, is very complex. There are people who literally don't have a home, but there's also a *lot* of people who actively choose this way of life. They want to live in complete freedom, without any rules, and much to my surprise, refuse government resources—relying instead on well-meaning people from the suburbs who are constantly bringing them clothing, food, medicine, and tents.

Since I know him, I start a dialogue. I've spent a lot of time talking with our homeless population, checking in on how they're doing, if there are any new people in their community who might be carrying weapons. Sometimes they'll give me information because they want to feel safe on the streets. Sometimes they just want to talk.

After a few minutes of back-and-forth, the man tells me why he wants to end his life.

"My girlfriend died," he says. "And I . . . I watched her die."

I talk with him some more, using all the skills I've learned to try to connect with him. I manage to break through his grief. We talk some more, and then he becomes cooperative. Officers escort him away, to take him to a hospital.

Someone retrieves his weapon. It's a BB gun. But it looks incredibly real.

Which isn't much of a surprise. A lot of homeless people carry BB guns and BB rifles for protection because they look so much like the real deal, and they're much cheaper—and easier—to acquire. We spent months searching for a man carrying an assault rifle, only to discover when we found him and searched his belongings that his "assault rifle" was, in fact, a BB gun.

There was no way to tell just by looking at it.

Fortunately, neither man was pointing their weapons at us when we located them. The outcomes might have turned out very, very differently.

There's a public misconception that all cops do is arrest people and take them to jail. The reality is that most of our calls involve civil matters. We help individuals dealing with mental illness get access to the resources and tools they need. We mediate disputes between neighbors, husbands and wives, parents and teenagers. People would be surprised by the number of calls we get from frustrated parents dealing with kids who won't listen to them. They want us to talk to their children.

I'm parking my car at the station when I meet a woman walking to the front door with a boy no older than five.

"Hey, ma'am, how can I help you?"

"I want you to arrest my son," she says.

I look around the parking lot, then back to her. "Where is he?"

She points to the boy standing next to her. He's gripping her leg, super scared.

"Why do you want me to arrest him?" I ask.

"He doesn't listen. He bites other kids. I don't know what to do anymore, and I've had enough. Take him to jail."

She wants me to instill fear, which is the worst thing you can do to a child. If he grows up scared of the police, he'll never call us if he or someone else needs help.

I take a knee and look at the boy. Smile.

He moves behind his mother.

"Hey, bud," I say softly. "I'm not going to take you to jail."

"I didn't ask you to talk to him," the mother says. "I told you to take him to jail."

"I'm not doing that."

She gets angry. I talk to her, try to get her to see reason, but she's not interested.

"Do your job!"

"Ma'am, I'm not taking your son to jail."

The woman walks away, furious.

I'm startled by the number of young people who have been

taught to fear the police and to never trust us, under any circumstances.

I came into this profession because I want to help people. Most cops do. Most times, our job involves seeing people at their worst. When we get a call, we don't care what you look like, we just want to help. When dealing with disputes, there will always be people who aren't happy with the end result, but the fact is, we *do* care.

The antipolice protests in the summer of 2020 and the ensuing riots remind me of riots back home. Only here, the protestors, many of whom flood in from other cities and states, surround our cars, preventing us from going out and doing our jobs. They call us racists and other hurtful things.

It's hard not to take it personally.

Protestors find out who we are and shout our names to the crowd. They know where we live. They encourage people to protest in front of our homes. I'm also a mom, and the idea of these protestors coming to my house is scary.

I grew up in a poor neighborhood, I want to tell these people. And when I came here, to this country, as a *foreigner,* I specifically chose to work in a similarly impoverished area because that was where I felt I belonged. Where I knew I could make a positive impact.

A concerned grandmother brings her four-year-old granddaughter to the station, worried that the girl might be a victim of parental abuse.

It's very hard to interview young children. They don't always remember dates and times clearly. I talk to the little girl. She's very sweet and innocent, and she's not scared as she answers my questions. She doesn't cry.

The interview is very long. When it's over, the little girl hands me a picture she drew while we talked. She gives me a big hug and says, "I want to be like you when I grow up."

Hearing those words, being able to help her—these are the kind of things that help give me the extra push I need to get through a bad day.

And today is a bad day, since now I have to go tell the grandmother she's right to be concerned.

"Your granddaughter has been sexually abused."

It's heartbreaking.

When I come home from work, I always hug my kids. I hug my kids extra hard that night. They're old enough to know what's going on in the world.

"I'm proud of you," they say.

That keeps me going.

RICHARD DILIBERTI

Richard Diliberti worked construction before entering the police academy shortly after he turned twenty.

An inmate sweeping the floor looks at my name tag and says, "Diliberti."

He's an older gentleman, clean-cut, very put-together. He also looks like a guy who's been in the system for a long time.

"You related to the Diliberti family from Long Island, New York?" he asks.

What's going on here?

I'm fresh out of the academy and this is my first day working as a trainee for the Los Angeles County Sheriff's Department, which has responsibility over the jail and court systems, and the transportation of prisoners. Trainees spend the first part of their careers working in the jail system.

It's important to build a rapport with the inmates, other cops have told me. *You're outnumbered a hundred to one, so you need to learn to be firm, but fair. Your reputation is what will allow you to survive.*

"What's your name?"

"Joe. You from New York?"

I nod. I was born in Queens and then my family relocated to California when I was young.

"I think I grew up with your uncle and your dad," he says.

I don't say anything, just nod and go about my business. While I'm checking in with the people I'll be working with, I ask one of the sheriffs, "That guy sweeping the hallway, who is he?"

He tells me the guy is the brother of a well-known mobster from my neighborhood. "He was a hit man for the mob. He's in here for multiple murders."

My dad grew up in Brooklyn during that time period, but he wasn't a part of that life. I call and tell him about Joe Hill.

"Yeah," he says, "me and your uncle grew up in Brooklyn with those guys."

My first day working in a jail that holds twenty thousand inmates and the first person I meet is a notorious mobster who knows my family.

This can't be good.

Or can it?

I decide to make the jail my education system. The inmates I work with are the kind of criminals who are hard to catch. I start interviewing them. *How did you become a criminal? What happened in your life that made you make these decisions?* I'm not trying to change them. I'm trying to obtain knowledge for when I eventually work patrol, so I can understand the streets, the people I'll be dealing with, where they came from.

One of my first assignments is to work what is arguably the highest level of security in the facility.

An inmate returning from a visit with his attorney is stabbed with a homemade weapon, what we call a shank. We find him bleeding out on the floor, nearly dead. The inmates in the surrounding cells are sitting on their bunks, acting like it's no big deal.

The attack was premeditated and took days, maybe even weeks to execute. Someone smuggled in a hacksaw blade to the inmate behind the attack, who used it to painstakingly cut away a section of the bars of his cell.

I learn that criminals think what they do is completely normal. It's as normal to them as working at a regular job, paying the bills, and taking care of our families feels to you and me.

I also learn that long-term change has to start at the family level. I work with guys who grew up on the same streets as these criminals. Some were raised by a single dad or mom who day by day showed them certain values and morals, a lifetime process outside the scope of teachers or correctional or police officers.

Patrol is where you earn your reputation, earn your bones. After six years working in the jail, I'm finally working patrol at South LA's Lennox Sheriff's Station. Drugs are rampant in the area, and there's a lot of street gang activity.

My job is very busy and unpredictable. It's not your typical nine-to-five job, and every day my schedule is up in the air. My job also has a very high element of danger—and that's my wheelhouse, what I like to do.

People can't understand how my wife, who stays at home to raise our two daughters, can be so supportive. "How do you deal with Rich's job?" they ask. "Don't you worry every time he leaves for work?"

"What am I supposed to do?" she always replies. "Stressing about it is exhausting. If something happens to him, I'm sure I'll be the first to know."

People don't really understand the dynamic of inner-city neighborhoods. The entire population is not out there committing crimes. The reality is, 90 percent of the people living there are simply hardworking people providing for their families. It's the 10 percent that are out there causing all the problems. My job is to protect the 90 and go after the 10.

I get dispatched to a house where a boy around six years old fell into a pool. The family pulled him out, and they couldn't get him to breathe.

The fire department is much better at resuscitation because that's a key part of their job. When my partner and I show up, we're the first ones on the scene. We immediately start CPR procedures to make sure the airway is open. Then we bring him out to the front so it will be easier for the fire department to get to us.

We're going through resuscitation efforts when the fire department arrives. They come in, take over, and transport him to the hospital. That afternoon, I arrive back at the station and see a bunch of news cameras out front. The mom is there. Her son survived, and she wanted to personally thank me and my partner.

Ten years later, I'm working on the SWAT team. We get a call for a hostage rescue, where we end up saving an elderly woman from a home invasion. A few team members and I are given a Medal of Valor, which is kind of cool for me and my family.

I don't want the pomp and circumstance and flag-waving. I'm just here to help. I'm just here to try to make things better—and people in the community appreciate that. To this day, I can be serving a search warrant in the Compton, and when I walk into a Starbucks, dressed in my SWAT gear, the staff will come out from the counter to give me a hug.

The mom whose son almost drowned tracks me down. "My son is graduating from high school. I want you to come to his graduation."

COREY GREEN

Corey Green works in the Maryland State Police Aviation
Command and flies medevac missions.

Most people think state troopers only do highway patrol, stop you for speeding. They don't know we have an aviation division. That we fly helicopters to save lives.

In this job, when I encounter kids in dangerous situations, I immediately think of my two children.

Today I'm treating a little girl who has been mauled by a dog. Her face is ripped off, and she's in a bad way by the time our helicopter lands in a nearby parking lot.

The EMS unit on the scene brings the girl to us. She's around my daughter's age, and as I'm tending to her, all I can think is *Man, this could be my kid.*

I quickly force that thought to the back of my mind. I have to, in order to focus effectively.

I get to work. The girl's airway needs to be secured, which means inserting a breathing tube. I give her medicine to sedate her, then insert the tube. Her body begins to relax, taking the physical stress off her heart. We pack her up and get her to the hospital.

She survives but will need a high level of care. She's lucky.

Not everyone is.

Shortly after 1 a.m., we get a call about a missing woman. She's elderly, has dementia, and is living with her son and his wife. She went to bed, dressed in her nightgown, and at some point, woke up, left the house, and wandered off.

It's the middle of the night, and it's snowing.

She's been missing for thirty minutes.

As we take off, I plug in the coordinates and recognize the address. It's not far from where I live.

Okay, think. If my mind wasn't clear and I was out wandering in the freezing cold, where would I go? What direction would I take?

The path of least resistance.

I turn to the pilot and say, "Let's search in and around the neighborhood first. Maybe she slipped and fell. It's pretty icy out."

We check some driveways and, sure enough, we find her lying down near the side of a house.

We radio the local cops. Now we need to find a place to land the helicopter.

We find a spot in the front yard of a neighboring house

across from where the victim fell. Our pilots are retired military pilots who flew in combat or flew in a presidential detail. They can drop us in some tight areas without difficulty.

We land. I quickly jump out. It's freezing cold, snow blowing everywhere.

The woman is dressed in her nightgown. No hat, scarf, or gloves. Her feet are bare. She's hypothermic. Her speech is slurred, she's confused, and she's suffered a head injury—a clear sign that she fell.

A couple of local cops have arrived. They look to me, expecting a break in procedure.

Usually in missions to locate a missing person with a medical condition, the ground units take control. But we can't wait for the ground medic to arrive. This woman needs to be transported to the trauma center, so we quickly transition from search and rescue to medevac.

I take over. I get her strapped up and loaded into the helicopter.

Once we deliver her to the hospital and get her taken care of, I track down the cell number for the woman's son and call to tell him about his mother.

"I can't thank you enough," he says.

TOM VENTO

Tom Vento is a veteran police officer.

Allen didn't show up for work today."
  The man on the other end of the line is Allen Howard's
boss and his neighbor. I know who Howard is because the
police were at his home last night.

  Howard is twenty-six and lives at home with his parents,
who are out of town for the next few days. He's despondent
over a recent breakup with his girlfriend. He confided in
a friend, who became concerned that Howard was possibly
suicidal and called the police. My sergeant went to Howard's
house, but Howard denied there was any problem, said his
friend overreacted.

  And now Howard's boss and neighbor is saying Howard
didn't show up to work today.

My sergeant and I arrive on-scene at the same time. It's winter, late evening, everything covered in a fresh blanket of snow. As we get the key from the next-door neighbor, I notice that there are no track marks in the snow around Howard's house. His car is covered in a good six inches. It hasn't been cleaned off.

That car's been sitting there all day.

I have a sick feeling in my stomach when I enter the house. I'm twenty-one years old and have been a cop for a little over a year.

We go room by room, turning on lights. In the TV room, we find a gun case and a box of cartridges on a table. When I move closer, I see a picture of a young woman.

Howard isn't anywhere on the first or second floors. My sergeant turns his attention to the basement door. He opens it and turns on a light.

I look down the set of stairs, see what looks like a scrap of flesh lying on the concrete floor.

We exchange looks.

This isn't going to be good.

Allen Howard is lying on a mattress. He's wearing two-piece flannel pajamas, like the kind my father has. His driver's license is next to him, on the floor. He drove a pencil through the back; the sharp lead tip sticks out from his forehead. He used the pencil as a stand, to prop up his license so it wouldn't be missed, possibly, or because he wanted to be easily identified. The rifle he used to kill himself has made a visual identification impossible. There's nothing left from the chin up.

I've seen fatalities before, but this one... I've never seen anything so graphic, or traumatic, in my life.

Twenty-six and he's wearing the same kind of pajamas my father and grandfather wear. Who wears pajamas at that age?

I don't know why I'm thinking about this.

My sergeant tells me to deliver the notification. Here I am, twenty-one years old, sitting at the family's rolling-top desk and calling the parents down in Florida to let them know what happened to their son.

I speak to Howard's father. I deliver the news and then listen to awful, inhuman sounds explode over the receiver.

I don't know what to say to console him.

The crime-scene tech arrives to take photos. He finds the bullet that exited Howard's head. It's lying on the floor.

"Hey, would you go over there and just point to the bullet so I can take a picture?" he asks me.

I walk over, feel something stuck to the bottom of my boot. I hear it scrape against the concrete floor.

I lift up my boot and see a tooth stuck into the lug sole. I pry it out using a pen.

"I need a break," I tell the tech.

He nods in understanding. "I've got to bag the guy's hands. How about you go back to the station and get me some paper bags."

It's late at night and snowing again. As I'm driving, I think about Howard killing himself over a breakup. It doesn't make any sense to me. I've been dumped and rejected a million times. It's never good, but I can't comprehend being distraught to the point where I'd want to kill myself.

Dispatch puts out a call about a car parked at a bank parking lot. "Snowplow drove by, said the vehicle's running and it looks like there's no one inside."

I hear the address. It's close to my current location. I radio dispatch and tell them I'll check on it.

I arrive and walk up to the car. It's still running, the heater on full blast. Lying sideways across the seat is an older woman. She's not wearing a winter jacket.

The car is unlocked. I open the door, check for a pulse. There isn't one. I call for an ambulance.

There's no blood and nothing to suggest the woman was attacked in any way. Her purse is inside the car. I open it, find her license. I run her name and then I find out she's the cleaning woman for the bank.

My best guess is she came out here to start her car and warm it up. At some point, she suffered a serious medical issue, like a heart attack or a stroke, and died.

I sit on the back bumper, in the freezing cold and snow, waiting for the ambulance. I think about this poor woman and Howard's father. The guttural sound he made when I told him his son was dead, and how he died. I think of Howard's tooth stuck in the sole of my boot.

The ambulance arrives. Steve, an ER doctor, is working tonight as a volunteer on the ambulance crew. After they get the dead woman squared away in the ambulance, Doc Bauer, as we call him, comes up to me and says, "You look rattled."

I tell him about my night.

"That's a lot to absorb," he says. "Tomorrow, there'll be an after-action review."

I know about AARs—these debriefs where officers involved in an incident discuss the actions they took at an incident, what they experienced, what things they could have done better. I've never been to one.

"You and everyone else who went to Howard's house should attend, talk about what you saw," he says. "Talking will help."

Will it? I like Doc Bauer. He's in his early thirties, cares about the community, and lives life on the edge. He's an adventurous guy, and eventually becomes a part-time police officer and SWAT medic.

My shift ends the following morning. I still live with my parents. I come home and tell them about the suicide, calling Howard's father—everything.

My mom and dad are good, kindhearted people, but they have no experience in law enforcement. They aren't equipped to offer their twenty-one-year-old son any guidance on this front.

"Go to bed," my mom says. "You'll feel better after you sleep."

What I've seen . . . it feels like I'm at a fork in the road. Either I'm going to deal with this, work through it and perform at my job, or I'm not.

I keep thinking of the tooth stuck in my boot.

When something like that happens, how do you go on and expect your life to go back to normal?

The pervasive attitude in law enforcement at the time is that cops don't go to counseling. Those who do are weak. If you do get help and cops find out, that information goes straight into your file—and word gets around the station. Cops needing help for mental health issues carry a stigma. They could end up shooting someone down the road, get their partner or another cop in a bad spot.

Real cops don't speak up. When you're hurt, you rub some dirt on it and get back in the game.

I don't agree with that mentality. And I respect Doc Bauer.

I attend the debrief. The evidence tech and I are the only cops who are there. Doc Bauer is here, along with a therapist, who encourages us to talk. I don't say too much, anxious to get back to work.

Two days after Howard's death, his parents send a deli tray of cold cuts and cheeses to the station, along with a note thanking us for being so compassionate.

I think about the crime scene. The last thing I want to eat is deli meat.

I go to roll call and hit the streets, completely unaware that the seed for PTSD has been planted.

I let it grow for ten years.

One night at home, my wife and I shut off the TV to get ready for bed. I leave the lights on downstairs, go upstairs, and turn on the lights for our bedroom and hallway. Then I return to the first floor, where I systematically turn off the lights in each room as I make my way back upstairs, to the bedroom.

"Why do you always do that?" my wife asks.

"Do what?"

"This thing with the lights," she says, describing what I just did.

I never noticed it before. "I don't know."

"You do it a lot. It's weird."

I think about it for a moment. Then I tell her about the incident with Allen Howard, his two-piece old-man flannel pajamas, the tooth stuck in my boot—all of it.

Then I realize something else. "This thing with the lights—I did it when I was living with my parents. My bedroom was in our refinished basement."

"You should talk to Amanda."

Amanda is our department's full-time social worker. She's a great woman, very approachable. One day I seek her out. I tell her about my unconscious ritual with the lights at home, how I think it might be connected to an incident I experienced when I was twenty-one. I tell her about Allen Howard.

"Are you familiar with EMDR?" she asks.

I shake my head.

"It's a type of psychotherapy," she says. "Stands for 'Eye Movement Desensitization and Reprocessing.' It helps people recover from trauma. Soldiers suffering from PTSD have used it with a lot of success."

She gives me a name. I make an appointment.

The therapist sits me down, tells me how EMDR is designed to allow the brain to resume its natural healing process. Unlike more conventional talk therapy, where you constantly revisit and discuss a traumatic event, EMDR allows you to process the trauma in fewer sessions, gently move past it so the brain will no longer be reacting in a fight-or-flight response.

Then she hands me a pair of headphones and has me look at this LED-type bar that's about two and a half feet long and about three inches wide. It's mounted on a camera tripod.

All I can see is a completely black background and a green ball of light that moves at a steady pace back and forth across the screen. Each time the green light hits one corner of the screen, I hear a little beep on my headphones.

It's the most bizarre thing I've ever seen.

"Okay," she says. "I want you to follow the light as you talk. Start from the time you pulled up at the house and walk me through the story."

I tell her the story.

"How long do you think that took?" she asks after I've finished.

"Ten minutes?"

"It was fifty. That means it's working. We'll see you again next week."

I do four more sessions. At the last one, I'm left with this feeling as though I've watched this twenty-one-year-old version of myself and the incident that haunted him—and me—get up from the couch and walk right out of my life.

Twenty-two years later, I go away for a guys' weekend. I share a mutual friend with the guy who owns the cabin: my buddy Brad. We grew up together, played Little League. I joined the police, and Brad and his two brothers became firefighters.

Brad and I are sitting around a bonfire. He turns to me and says, "How do you deal with your PTSD?"

I'm taken aback by his question. Why does he assume I have PTSD?

He starts talking about a local mass shooting involving a man who had recently been served a restraining order in court. His wife was afraid for her life and wanted a divorce. The judge ordered him to stay away from his wife for the next four years.

Three days later, the guy walked into the high-end salon and spa where his soon-to-be ex-wife worked and opened fire with a .40-caliber handgun, killing her and two other female employees. He wounded four others before turning the weapon on himself. He died of a self-inflicted gunshot wound.

As commander of our SWAT team, I responded to the call. Eight other SWAT teams from neighboring cities and towns were also deployed. Nearly 150 law enforcement officers were there that day.

As Brad and I talk, it dawns on me that the fire and paramedic personnel were just as involved as the police were that day. I hadn't ever really stopped and thought about the important role they play as first responders—that they, too, are thrown into gruesome events and, afterward, are left to find ways to deal with their emotions.

I share my experiences with EMDR with him.

Over my three decades of being a cop, I only know one guy who was shot and killed in the line of duty. I know five cops who shot and killed themselves.

And the tragic thing? The signs were there.

Cops put out daily fires and inject themselves into the lives of people involved in the court system, but we don't inject ourselves when we see potential mental health issues with our coworkers. We see signs and don't want to believe that a problem exists. *He/she will be fine,* we say.

For the longest time, our profession hasn't done enough to take care of our people. The stats keep saying that more officers are dying from suicide than from felonious assault.

But it's getting better. I'm seeing more traction in terms of addressing mental health issues. There are a lot of police officer support groups. Some agencies are making it mandatory that their people seek counseling once a year—and they'll pay you to do it. Whether you talk or not is up to you.

JOE MAURIELLO

Joe Mauriello is a veteran of the Cook County Sheriff's Police Department.

The guy isn't answering his door.

It's early evening, and all the drapes and shades in the house are already drawn.

I'm here responding to a burglary call made by the owner of the house.

I knock again on the front door, wait.

Still no answer.

I'm twenty-four and have only been on the job for four months, but I know this is weird. I go around to the back door, knock, and when no one answers, I walk back to my squad car, my thoughts turning to a recent late-night call I made to another house here in the Chicago area.

I identify myself, then ask, "May I come in?"

"Is everything okay?" a woman answers. It's after two in the morning and she's half asleep.

"I regret to inform you that your husband was in a fatal car crash." My tone is official—not cold, but lacking in bedside manner. "He hit a sheet of ice, ran off the road, and crashed into a tree."

I stand there helpless as the woman drops to the floor, crying.

That was the moment I learned that as a police officer, I don't have all the answers. That I'm not as powerful—or as helpful—as I think I am.

I open the door to the squad car and call the radio room.

"I knocked on the front door twice and the back door once and no answer," I say. "Either this guy isn't home, or he's not answering the door."

I'm told to wait. It's hot out, so I crank up the air conditioning.

The radio room calls back and says, "The homeowner is coming to the front door now."

The man is five ten, stocky, dressed for work in a collared shirt and pants. He has a mustache and his thick salt-and-pepper hair is parted on the side. He is friendly and apologetic for not being here when I arrived. He had left some paperwork at a neighbor's house and went to retrieve it.

I enter his dimly lit house, the waning sunlight barely penetrating the drawn blinds. He takes me to a bedroom converted into a home office, starts to explain why he called in a burglary.

While he was out to dinner with his wife and family, one of his business partners—he's not sure which one, exactly—came into his office and stole some contracts and other important documents. The thief left before he got back.

I look at the architectural drawings on the wall and say, "Is this what you do for a living?"

He nods. "I own a construction company."

I pull out my notebook to take down his information. "Your name?"

"John Wayne Gacy." He hands me his business card. "If you ever need any work done on your place, let me know."

A year later, I'm working as part of a ten-person tactical unit. It's late December, and I'm on vacation when I get a call from my boss.

"I'm sure you know what's going on with John Wayne Gacy," he says.

I do. Gacy has become a major national news story.

It started with the disappearance of a local boy.

When police executed a search warrant on December 13, they found shackles, handcuffs—and a class ring belonging to a missing teenager from another state. That prompted a new search warrant, which led to the discovery of a set of human remains buried in the crawl space of Gacy's home.

More digging in the crawl space has revealed two more sets of remains. No one knows how many bodies could be buried there or in other parts of the house. And Gacy won't say.

"The search warrant," my boss says, "the way it's written up, it's null and void the moment the last police officer leaves the property. You're going to be assigned to Gacy's house until further notice."

My partner and I will work a twelve-hour shift—11 p.m.

to 11 a.m. When we arrive at the house, we're taken to the back room—the family room, what Gacy calls his playroom. It's nearly empty. The pool table, entertainment equipment, and most of the furniture have been replaced with people and the gear they need to excavate and collect human remains.

I set up a blanket and a chaise longue—the folding ones for catching some sun on your patio—in the middle of the room. I don't want to sit anywhere near a wall covered in blood, spit, God only knows what else.

It's winter. The house is drafty, and the heat has been turned off. I wrap my blanket around me and stare down at the hole leading to the crawl space. It's all muddy and full of clay, and the cold air blowing up at me reeks to high hell.

I've never smelled a dead body before, let alone several.

It's the longest, creepiest night of my life.

The next morning, at 6:30 a.m., investigators and contractors arrive at the house and get to work in the crawl space. Some investigators go through Gacy's freezer and take out unmarked packages of what appears to be ground beef.

Or is it human?

For the next several days, I watch them pull out more remains from the crawl space. I think about how helpless I felt when I informed that unsuspecting woman her husband had died, and I feel helpless now, knowing that there isn't anything I can do for these victims or their families.

Each night, I sit in my chaise longue, tallying up the bodies removed from the crawl space. The number climbs to eight.

Then twelve.

Fifteen.

How many more bodies could possibly be buried in the crawl space?

When they're finished, the final number is twenty-six.

They find three more bodies buried outside Gacy's home.

Investigators return their attention to the interior of the house. Police pull up the floors, knock down walls—they're tearing the house down room by room, searching for more remains, evidence, anything.

They find one last victim. The remains are buried in the concrete floor of the playroom—directly underneath my chaise longue.

RACHEL TOLBER

Rachel Tolber first learned about crime-scene investigations interning with a homicide detective. Rachel works on the West Coast as a commander for patrol and community services.

I arrive at the scene. A young male has overdosed on heroin. He's surrounded by EMTs and firemen, and isn't moving or breathing.

It's my first time seeing an OD up close, but I'm pretty sure he's dead.

A fireman administers Narcan, a drug that reverses the effects of an opioid overdose. Seconds later, the guy's eyes fly open.

He jumps up and starts fighting.

I can't believe what I'm seeing.

It takes several people to subdue him. As we restrain him and then bring him to the ambulance, so he can get treatment, I can't stop thinking about how I saw someone literally come back from the dead.

Overdoses from heroin and other street and prescription drugs have become a huge problem, especially around the holidays. I get called to many scenes where victims can't be revived. The emotional devastation their families and children go through—it's heartbreaking.

In my line of work, I come across all sorts of people, and while there's a good chance I may never know if I had a positive impact on them or not, if I treat them with respect, there's always hope. And if I can help one person, then I can hope he or she will go on to help others too.

In early 2000, my department creates a program to help people on parole reenter society. I put in for the police position and end up working with a good friend, a drug-court liaison officer. I go with him to do home checks and deal with parolees.

Today, I'm dealing with a parolee named Jimmie. He's a smart guy, works as an electrician. He's also addicted to meth and has a long criminal record dealing drugs. I enter his home with the parole agents to conduct a search and administer a drug test.

Jimmie is clearly high. "I can't do a urine test today," he says.

"Why not?"

"Because I can't pee. I'm not feeling well."

He starts listing excuses. I cut him off.

"Look, how about having just an ounce of respect for your parole agent and the rest of us," I say. "We all know you're high, okay? You're not the only person we're working with today, so just tell the truth so we can all move on."

He glares at me for a moment, then he reaches up to the drop ceiling and moves a tile out of the way.

Oh, crap, I've pushed this too far. He's going to grab a gun.

"Whoa," I say. "What are you doing?"

Jimmie removes a meth pipe. Hands it to me.

"You're right," he says. "I got high earlier this morning."

We end up arresting him for being under the influence and for having drug paraphernalia, both clear parole violations. We take him to jail. When he goes to court, we ask the judge if we can take him to drug court, which allows addicts to go into treatment programs. If the addict completes the program, gets work, stays clean, and successfully graduates, then the case will be closed and cleared.

The judge agrees, and Jimmie is accepted into a treatment program. The rest is up to him.

A decade later, I get a call at the station. It's Jimmie.

"I'm getting my ten-year coin," he tells me. "Would you come to my AA meeting?"

I attend the meeting and listen to the speech Jimmie gives. He's now married to a woman who works with people suffering from substance abuse, and he goes to schools to talk to kids about his experiences with addiction and how they led to the choices that landed him in prison.

"The last time I was arrested, I would have said or done anything to stay out of jail," Jimmie says. Then he points to me. "Officer Tolber treated me with respect. She made me realize I'm responsible for my own actions, but she also wanted to help me. She took me to drug court and helped get me into a program where I finally got clean."

Jimmie's family is there. After the ceremony is over, his son comes up and thanks me. "You gave us our dad back."

Jimmie gives me his ten-year chip.

I carry it with me as a reminder that people *can* change.

LOU DELLI-PIZZI

Lou Delli-Pizzi is a veteran of the New York City Police Department.

It's evening. The streets are crowded. I'm standing at the front door of a smoke shop, acting as a deterrent to neighborhood drug crime, when I hear multiple gunshots.

A big guy runs past the door, firing a gun over his shoulder.

I dart outside. Remove my sidearm and order him to freeze and drop his weapon.

He keeps running. I chase after him.

Get so close I tackle him.

I wrestle the gun away, then manage to subdue him quickly. It isn't much of a fight, and the guy isn't injured in any way. For evidence, I literally have a smoking gun and spent shells lying a couple of feet away.

I bring him to the station. He waives his Miranda rights. After I have him printed, I let him use the bathroom, then take him, handcuffed, to the muster room, where we get our assignments and intelligence briefings. Another cop guards him while I go over to the vending machines.

A patrol cop asks me what I'm doing. I say I'm going to try to talk to him.

"Don't bother," he says. "We're not detectives, let them handle that."

Anyone I arrest, I treat with basic human decency: bring them to the bathroom, give them cigarettes, even buy them food. It helps to build trust. I want to see if I can gather some intelligence—find out where he got the gun, the name of the person he was trying to shoot.

I start dropping quarters into the vending machine. The patrol cop knows what I'm doing.

"That food is for us," he says.

I ignore him. I bring the shooter a soda and a Hostess apple pie. He's a young guy, maybe early twenties. He appears very relaxed. We get to talking, and he tells me his name is Ostin, and he's originally from the Dominican Republic.

I keep asking who he was trying to shoot, and Ostin keeps saying, "Some guy with red hair."

I try to engage him in further conversation, but his English is limited. I don't get much in the way of crucial information from him.

"Is there anyone you want to call?" I ask.

"My wife."

"Where is she?"

"Hospital. Having baby."

"All right, which hospital?"

He's not sure. Ostin gives me his wife's name. I call a couple of places but come up empty.

Later, I bump into a friend and tell him about my arrest. "I literally found him with a smoking gun," I say.

"That's great, Lou. Case like that will never go to trial."

The next day, an attorney shows up. He's going around the neighborhood, talking to people. His name is Brad Jones. I've seen him around the courthouse.

Jones is straight out of central casting. Capped teeth and perfect hair, flashy suits and expensive silk ties. Showy and obnoxious as hell. He's *the* lawyer for a major drug cartel.

Our postarrest investigation reveals that Ostin is known to be a drug-dealing lieutenant in this neighborhood.

The case ends up going to a jury trial.

Because Ostin has no prior arrests, we can't introduce him as a "drug lieutenant" since this information would be considered hearsay.

Jones takes an unusual tack. He serves what's called a late alibi notice, stating the defendant wasn't actually even present at the crime scene. He lists names of the corroborating witnesses. The presentation of an alibi notice is typically timed to allow police and prosecutors to investigate its claims. But the trial is already in progress.

The judge allows it.

I'm the sole police witness. A rookie cop. This neighborhood doesn't have surveillance cameras. It's my word against Ostin's.

Ostin's wife takes the stand. "I was eating dinner at a restaurant with my husband," she tells the court. "Someone was firing a gun, and my husband got up and went outside to see what was going on. Then this brutal cop beats him up and tries to put my husband's hand on this gun, so his fingerprints are on it."

A waitress working at the restaurant that night is the next to testify. "Ostin is a great customer, a good tipper. He was eating dinner with his wife. Some other person was firing a gun, and then I saw this cop beating Ostin up and trying to put Ostin's fingerprints on the gun."

Jones addresses the court. "What we have here is yet another example of police brutality."

A few jury members nod in agreement.

My stomach drops. I feel myself separating from my body. *This can't be happening.*

A restaurant patron further states that I planted evidence on Ostin and that he was, in fact, eating dinner with his wife. The patron calls Ostin a wonderful man and upstanding citizen. Jones plays it up, saying he'll be talking to the US attorney, that there'll be a federal prosecution.

I didn't do this, I want to scream. *I made a solid arrest, recovered a smoking gun and the spent shells. These witnesses are lying.*

And the jury, I'm sensing from their body language, is swept up in antipolice sentiment on the rise in the city because of recent incidents in the news.

We don't have much time left in trial. I pull the DA aside and say, "These people are lying. I think I can prove it."

"How?"

"Day I arrested Ostin, he told me his wife was having a baby. If you issue some subpoenas, I'll hit every hospital, try to find a record of this woman giving birth."

The DA gives me the subpoenas. I go out and investigate.

I find the hospital where Ostin's wife had their baby, secure her medical records.

It's the last day of trial. I bring the documents with me to court. The DA reintroduces me as a rebuttal witness.

The judge gives me a stern but curious look through his small round glasses. A look that says, *What's this guy going to come up with?*

"Officer," the DA says to me, "did you conduct an investigation in the last forty-eight hours?"

"Yes, I did."

"And what did you find?"

The jury's attention is locked on me.

"The defendant's wife was in a hospital giving birth at the time of the shooting arrest," I say. "Here are the hospital records."

In TV legal dramas, there's always some big Perry Mason moment. That doesn't happen in real life. There's no jury gasping in surprise or judge hammering a gavel on the block, calling for order. But everyone in the courtroom is in shock.

Jones gets to his feet. "Your Honor, I'd like to talk to my client outside the courtroom and discuss a possible plea deal."

Ostin is out on bail. The judge says, "You can talk to your client, but it won't be outside of this courtroom. He'll be in a holding cell. He's now a flight risk."

After Ostin is convicted, we reinterview his alibi witnesses. Every single one gives up the attorney. Every single one is locked up for perjury.

All because I bought a soda and a Hostess apple pie.

It's the best money I've ever spent.

AMY DEHNER

Lieutenant Colonel Amy Dehner is the chief deputy director for the Michigan State Police.

I've pulled over an old farming truck because one of its tail-lights is out. It's evening, dark. The driver is a big fella—probably around six foot eight and well over three hundred pounds. He's so big that his chest is touching the steering wheel and the top of his head hits the cab's roof.

With traffic stops, the driver and officer are both in a state of heightened awareness. Knowing how to communicate to control a situation is what sets good cops apart from bad cops.

I tell him why I pulled him over, then ask why he isn't wearing his seat belt.

"Because seat belts are garbage," he replies, and launches

into a story about a car crash he was in, how the only reason he survived, his doctor told him, was because he *wasn't* wearing a seat belt.

His voice keeps rising as he gets into specifics of the crash. His face is red and he's sweating, and he keeps touching his legs and fiddling with the seat belt, or maybe the window, which is open a quarter of the way.

When you do enough traffic stops, you get a sense of things. My gut says he's not reaching for a gun or a weapon. He's fidgeting because he's angry, and he's staring straight out the front window.

Still, I'm trying to keep an eye on his hands when he tells me he's so big he can't wear a seat belt. Then, as if he wants to prove just how big he really is, he tries to open the door.

I keep a hand on it, so the door remains shut.

While I'm tall for a woman—six feet two inches and 160 pounds—if this guy decides to get out of the truck, I'm going to have a serious problem.

And I'm the only car on duty. The sheriff's car is tied up on a call on the other side of the county.

The driver is getting louder, angrier. The veins are bulging along his head.

Before I became a police officer, I got a college degree in sports management, then played professional basketball in Switzerland for two seasons. I traveled all over Europe, and when I returned home, I joined the Army. I'm thankful I became a trooper at a later age. I feel like it made me a little more mature, more patient.

Just let him talk.

He pauses to take a breath. Now's my chance to speak.

"Hey, look," I say calmly. "I understand that you were in a crash once and your doctor told you, oh, it's a good thing you weren't wearing a seat belt because you would've been killed."

His gaze slides to mine.

"Let me tell you about my job, what I see every day," I say. "I've never been to a car accident like the one you just described. All the calls I go to, when someone isn't wearing a seat belt—that person gets ejected from the car. Either that person is killed instantly, or he gets thrown underneath a vehicle and crushed to death."

I've got his full attention now.

Compassion, more times than not, can win the day. I say, "I'm not here to ruin your day. You have a family somewhere, and I'm sure they'd like to see you again."

My words hit home. His body immediately relaxes.

"Yeah," he says, letting out a long sigh. "Yeah, you're right." He laughs at himself at bit, shakes his head. "I was getting really worked up."

"I know you were. And, honestly, I didn't know what I was going to do with you."

We both laugh a little. The situation quickly de-escalates. I ask him about his missing rear plate. He says he had no idea it was missing.

I tell him I'm not giving him a ticket for not wearing a seat belt. He promises to get his taillight fixed.

With traffic stops, my department always needs a little give-and-take so our troopers can, hopefully, get to a positive outcome in certain situations. We'll only get to that place if we communicate patiently.

KEITH BROUGHTON

*Keith Broughton has worked as a patrolman, a detective, a
detective sergeant, and a patrol supervisor.*

The fire is out of control, threatening to engulf the entire
apartment building, one of several fourplex units in the
public housing area. Thick black smoke churns through all
the broken windows while I, along with other police officers
and state troopers, try to keep the people back.

The fire, I've been told, originated in one of the first-floor
apartments. It belongs to two people I went to high school
with, Barbara and Dale. They have two kids—a pair of boys,
ages ten and twelve.

A few short hours ago, Barbara left her kids in the apartment and went to borrow something from a neighbor in a
building across the street. She wasn't gone but five minutes,

but when she returned home, she saw flames in the front living room windows and screamed for help.

Barbara, thinking of her sons, opened the front door to her apartment. The outside air rushed in and blew her back into the street as her neighbors opened the back door, inadvertently creating a funnel that fueled the fire.

Her two boys are nowhere outside, which leads us to believe they're trapped somewhere inside the building.

I see Dale, the father, charging across the yard, heading straight for the firefighters who are standing on the apartment's front porch, trying to put out the flames. The look of fear and determination on his face tells me he's going to go charging right into those flames to try and save his kids.

A trooper and I tackle Dale only a few feet from the doorway.

Later, after the fire is put out, two bodies are discovered inside the bedroom.

I know I did the right thing, keeping Dale from rushing inside the building. If I didn't, he would have died. But no matter how hard I try, I can't stop thinking about how I tackled a father to the ground to prevent him from saving his babies.

Tim is in trouble all the time. He's out on bond and he decides to go out and get drunk. He gets into a fight with a guy named Ben—and Ben absolutely whips Tim's ass.

When I pull into the parking lot of the housing area where both men live, I see Tim chasing after Ben.

Ben runs past my car. I get out, looking at Tim, who is coming dead at me—and he's holding a two-by-four and a butcher knife above his head.

This is the second time I've had to pull my weapon. The first time, I was fighting with a guy who decided to pull a knife on me. I was milliseconds away from pulling the trigger when he stopped fighting me and decided to comply.

Training kicks in as I look down the target sight, at Tim, and scream, *"Stop!"*

Tim doesn't slow. I scream at him again to stop, and Tim keeps charging at me.

I slide my finger inside the trigger guard. I keep screaming, Tim keeps running, and now I have no choice.

I put my finger on the trigger.

Tim comes to a sudden stop about fifteen feet away from me.

As I get him down on the ground, all I can think about is how glad I am that I didn't have to pull the trigger.

Right then, in that moment, all I want to do is to go home and see my family.

I sit down inside an interview room with a state police detective and look across the table at a man who is guilty of raping his own children.

We get to talking, and the guy says, "Well, they're my kids. I ought to be able to do with them what I want."

I want to get up and beat his ass until I kill him. The detective, I know, feels the exact same way.

I stay involved in my kids' lives, go to every single one of their sporting events. And I believe in our justice system. You've got to do what the system says even though you don't always agree with it.

On a Friday afternoon, I get a call from one of the state police lab technicians.

"Your rapist," she says. "I know who he is."

Nearly eight years ago, I was involved in a case where a woman was raped at knifepoint in her home while her children slept across the room, in their beds. Another victim followed two weeks later, and two weeks after that, in another county, a fourteen-year-old cheerleader was raped in the bathroom during a basketball game.

All three victims gave the same description of their attacker.

When I started working the cases, I discovered two additional victims who lived nearby, in Lawrenceburg and Lexington.

I call the first victim and say, "We have him. I'm getting an arrest warrant."

The father from the Lawrenceburg case called us a lot, asking for updates on his daughter's case. I grab the case file, get his phone number, and give him a call. His voice mail picks up. I leave a message for him and his wife, saying I have some information and to call me back.

He does, on Monday. "My wife and I were out of town," he says. "We came home Sunday night, and when we heard your message saying you wanted to talk to us, we both knew why you called. You found him, didn't you?"

"We did."

"I knew it." The relief in his voice is palpable. "Sunday, my wife and I were celebrating our anniversary. Hearing your message, we couldn't have gotten a better gift."

The day before New Year's Eve is brutally cold. At one in the morning, I stop for coffee inside a local gas station convenience store. The curly, dark-haired woman working behind the counter is probably somewhere in her early twenties but looks younger.

Her name is Meredith. I don't know her personally, but I grew up with her family, went to school with her uncles. I know her grandparents.

"Did you pick somebody up earlier on Rose Hill?" she asks.

"She was walking alone, and I asked her if she wanted a ride home." I don't know her name, just where she lives.

"That was my little sister," Meredith says. "Thank you so much for giving her a ride. It's really cold out there."

"No problem."

Half an hour later, I'm parked alongside a state trooper and we're talking when dispatch calls about a robbery alarm going off at a convenience store—the same one where I picked up my coffee.

When we arrive, I see my brother-in-law, who works as a patrolman for the police department, is already there, walking toward the front door. He opens it, steps back, and pulls out his gun.

Cash registers are equipped with bills attached to sensors that, when triggered, alert the alarm company. The register has been wiped out, but nothing else inside the store has been disturbed.

And there's no sign of Meredith.

I quickly learn that she didn't return home and, fearing the worst, begin a search.

Six hours later, the morning sun climbing steadily in the clear blue winter sky, all I can think about is how my brother-in-law told me that he pulled into the convenience store parking lot thirteen seconds after the robbery alarm went off.

If something happened to Meredith, it was fast.

We get a call from a lady who says there's a body in her driveway. The address is less than ten miles away. I arrive and find Meredith lying dead on a rural road.

She's been brutally murdered.

The Kentucky State Police send their best homicide investigator. We work together with the FBI and police agencies in eleven other states as we chase down various leads.

Year after year passes, and we still can't find her killer.

Growing up and living in Versailles, I've gotten to know the majority of people who live here. Seeing Meredith's family nearly every day and knowing there isn't anything I can do for them—it's hard. I know how frustrated and angry they are. I talk to them about it.

"I want you to understand that we have done everything we can do—and it's not just us. The state police and the FBI, they've done everything, too. I know you're disappointed."

I am, too, I add privately. Not being able to give closure to the family and the community on a brutally heinous murder—it eats me up. Every time I go by that driveway where I found her, I see her lying there. The wounds and blood.

I think about her all the time, can't stop thinking about her.

I tell my doctor. He urges me to see a counselor. I do, and I end up talking about Meredith. I also tell him about how, for the past twenty-five years, I think about how I stopped that father from rushing inside his house to save his babies. How I would cry like a little kid because of the guilt and pain I felt over doing the right thing.

Cops and soldiers, sometimes we're put into positions where we see things no human being should ever see. No matter how strong you are, down the road, it comes back and haunts you.

As a patrol supervisor, I tell my people the critical importance of being polite.

"If you start out being rude or a butthead, there's no way to go but down. And keep in mind that the vast amount of people in this country have never had contact with a police officer on a personal level. That very first impression of you is what they're going to think about all nine hundred thousand of us, so be polite."

Our police department has a program that helps raise money to take less fortunate kids out Christmas shopping. It helps us build a good rapport with these children so, as they grow up, they don't see the police as people who just show up to drag away or arrest Mommy and Daddy.

The Saturday before Christmas, I drive out to the public housing area and knock on the front door. A woman answers the door. I tell her I'm here to pick up her son to go Christmas shopping.

The boy walks up and introduces himself. His name is Clyde, and he's seven.

"Here," he says, and gives me a handful of change. "I know you guys are going to spend a lot of money today, so I wanted to help."

I damn near choke up right there. The gesture reaffirms my belief that if you do good for people, good things will happen to you.

BRAD WAGNER

Brad Wagner is a police lieutenant in Washington, DC.

I get a call about a suicide. When I arrive at the house, the distraught family is gathered in the living room. The son, who is in his late twenties, shot and killed himself in his upstairs bedroom.

When I go upstairs, I find a hysterical man in the victim's bedroom.

"My son!" he screams. "Please help my son!"

The father's holding a handgun. I don't feel threatened—he's not pointing the weapon at me, just holding it.

I glance at the bed, at a young adult male lying on top of the comforter. He has a bloody pillowcase over his head. It's obvious that he's been shot in the head. The father is holding the weapon his son used to kill himself, I'm assuming.

"Help him. Help my son."

"Sir, I need you to hand me the gun."

The man gives it over to me. Screaming through his tears, he begs me again and again to help his son.

"Sir, he's dead," I say. "There's nothing I can do."

I'm numb to the situation, to what's happening. I work in the busiest district, on the busiest shift. Death, unfortunately, is a common occurrence.

The detective sergeant shows up.

"What do we have?" he asks me.

"A dead guy." My tone is matter-of-fact.

The dead man, I find out, shot and killed his girlfriend in another part of the district. Then he came home and killed himself. So now we're dealing with two homicides.

In some counties, an officer might get one homicide a year and maybe a shooting once a month. I get at least one homicide a week. Every day, I'm dealing with shootings, stabbings, burglaries, domestic disputes, and drug slingers who terrorize neighborhoods.

The violence and death never stop. It just goes on and on and on. Every year, it gets worse. Every day, I feel like a soldier on a battlefield.

It's insane.

After I clear the crime scene, I keep replaying it in my head. What bothers me is my tone of voice. It's cold. I handle the scene as though I'm working an auto theft report. I'm ashamed of my lack of compassion and empathy. My callousness.

When I started out, I was such an idealist. I would attend community meetings and discuss crime numbers. My first meeting, I approached the podium, introduced myself, and said, "I'm a police officer, not a politician, so I may not come across as polished. But I promise to tell you the truth."

The community loved my honesty and authenticity. They loved knowing I wasn't going to blow smoke up their ass.

I had such high hopes.

God, what's become of me?

I'm losing my humanity.

I'm out patrolling an inner-city neighborhood at night. A lot of people who live here—especially young men—don't want to have anything to do with the police. I've gone out of my way to try to get to know them, have a civilized conversation, but every time I get out of my car and approach them, they always walk away.

Don't talk to the police, ever. That's the predominant culture here and in many other inner-city neighborhoods. *Don't talk to the police and don't be nice to them. And never, under any circumstances, trust them.* They hate us, yet they're calling 911 all the time for help.

I roll into a block of brick-faced homes and small lawns sectioned off by chain-link fences and see a group of older people and some women running toward my car, yelling, "They shot him, they shot him!"

I get on the radio. "I'm being told someone got shot," I tell the dispatcher, and then relay my location.

I find a man in a red jacket lying facedown on the ground, with several entry wounds on his back. I find the gun, literally smoking, a few feet away.

The scene is chaotic. People are standing around watching, some are screaming in grief and fear. My focus narrows on the shooting victim.

I quickly ascertain he's dead, then get to work taping off the crime scene. I'm the only one here. By the time my backup arrives, the crowd has mostly dissipated. Any potential witnesses have left.

Later, after months of investigation, I'll learn that the shooter had stood in the crowd, watching. Todd Robinson. Robinson is a well-known fixture in the neighborhood—a very bad guy, wanted for a lot of crimes. But we can never find any evidence or witnesses to charge him.

I don't know why Robinson stuck around. Maybe he wanted to be sure the victim was dead. Maybe he thought, *If I take off running, that automatically makes me suspicious, and the cop will chase me. But if I stay here and act like I'm a part of the crowd...*

That night, no one at the scene pointed to Robinson and said, "Here's the shooter." No one in the neighborhood was going to snitch on him. We fail to uncover any evidence to tie him to the shooting. No witnesses come forward.

Years later, I'm called back to that same block to deal with a man who has been shot in the groin. The crotch of his jeans is blood-soaked, and he's in incredible pain.

"The ambulance is on its way," I tell him. "Who shot you?"

"I'm not telling you, man."

"Come on. I might be the last person you ever talk to."

The reality of his situation hits home.

"Robinson," he says.

"Todd Robinson?"

"Yeah. Him. He's the one who shot me."

The ambulance arrives and rushes him to the hospital. The victim lives. Detectives quickly find out the guy is part of Robinson's crew. He disrespected a higher-ranked member and Robinson put out a kill order—except the guy survived.

Detectives go to the hospital and talk to the victim.

"No." The victim backpedals. "I never said Robinson shot me."

The crime scene doesn't yield any useful evidence, and because the victim recants, we can't charge Robinson.

Todd Robinson's failed kill order saves him. Had the victim died, what he said to me could have been used as what's called a dying declaration. We could have arrested Robinson, and he most likely would have been convicted at trial and imprisoned. Lives would have been saved.

But it doesn't work out that way. Robinson is never jailed or brought to trial.

JAMES McSORLEY

James McSorley works as a detective supervisor on the West Coast.

A 911 call comes in coded "unknown trouble," meaning that police response is requested but without clear or specific reason.

The primary unit is already at work when my partner and I arrive as backup at an upscale residence built for privacy on a spacious lot at the edge of the Hollywood Hills.

In the back, I find a sliding glass door. It's open.

My partner calls my name. When I reach him near the side of the house, he points to a large, ornate window and says, "Take a look."

The view through the window is a living room that flows into an open kitchen.

A naked male is lying on the floor. He's not moving, clearly dead. There's blood everywhere—spray patterns all over the walls and furniture—but it's the state of his murdered body that shocks me. The victim was brutally beaten. The weapon, I suspect, is the fireplace poker that's sticking out of his chest.

To be killed in such horrific fashion, with such fury, is disturbing in any instance—but it's especially unexpected here. Stuff like this doesn't happen in the Hollywood Hills. Ever.

We access the house and begin to clear the residence.

When I reach the living room, I find the man's clothes. They're also covered in blood. Based on what I'm seeing, the clothes seem to have been forcibly removed from the body, possibly after he was unconscious. Or already dead.

My initial assumption that the victim was beaten to death with the fireplace poker turns out to be wrong. Nearby, I find a meat cleaver and several kitchen knives. Multiple stab wounds to the face and body have rendered the victim unrecognizable.

I glance to the kitchen. There's clear evidence of a struggle. We resume our search of the home.

Upstairs, I turn the corner and step into the main bedroom, where I discover an even more disturbing scene. A man's severed head is on the bed, a belt wrapped around the mouth. The dead man's eyes are staring directly at me.

Now we're dealing with two victims.

We clear the rest of the house, find no signs of the suspect. We set up a crime scene, call in the cavalry, and secure the perimeter.

The victim in the living room, we discover, is Dr. Albert Bird. While Homicide deals with the crime scene, I assist in interviewing the neighbors.

Los Angeles is a car-based culture. Everyone is always driving somewhere and as a result people don't get to really know their neighbors all that much. The people I talk to don't know Dr. Bird personally, but they all tell me warm and glowing stories about the man—how Bird went out of his way to help people in need. He gave back to the community through charity work and donated a lot of his time to mentoring young people—especially troubled teenagers, doing whatever he could to help turn their lives around. He also made it a priority to help people in the community who couldn't afford health care and medications.

Every single person I later interview describes the doctor as an exceptional human being. A leader and a mentor.

A short while later, we get another 911 call. It comes from a woman who's only a few streets away.

Another dead body has been discovered.

My partner and I arrive at a ranch-style house. An older woman stands outside. She looks to be somewhere in her eighties.

"Do you live here, ma'am?" I ask.

She shakes her head. Her face is white as a sheet. Her eyes are wide, and she's having trouble standing. It's clear she's in a state of shock.

"No," she replies, her voice barely above a whisper. "My boyfriend."

"What about your boyfriend?"

"He lives here. It's his house. He gave me a key. I opened the door and went inside ..."

"Ma'am?"

She opens her mouth to speak and a look of horror washes across her face.

She can't talk.

Another officer stays with the woman while my partner and I approach the house. We need to clear the residence.

I open the front door.

"What the hell?" my partner says.

The air is thick with steam—so thick that I can barely see enough to make out the rooms. I move inside carefully. It's hot and suffocating. My clothes stick to my skin. It's like that scene from the movie *Insomnia* where Al Pacino, playing an LAPD detective, searches for the killer inside a fog so thick he can't see his hand in front of his face.

And now my partner and I are going to hunt for a real-life killer inside one big steam room.

As we inch forward, our weapons drawn, we hear running water.

Why would the killer turn on all the hot water?

Did he leave, or is he still inside the house?

Is he hiding somewhere?

What the hell is going on?

I'm moving down a narrow hall, drenched in sweat, when I spot a pair of bare legs sticking out from the door to a bathroom. I move closer. A male body lies on the floor. He's been savagely stabbed to death. Completely massacred.

And his head is missing.

*   *   *

Detectives end up retrieving multiple fingerprints from the crime scenes. They belong to Stephen Dylan, a man with a well-documented history of drug use and mental illness.

Police hold a press conference. Dylan is their prime suspect. They show the most recent photo they have of him and ask the public for help.

Calls come in quickly. When Dylan is located, he's sitting on a park bench, holding a can of pepper spray and a bouquet of handpicked wildflowers.

Dylan is arrested. On the day of the murders, he admits to having been high on methamphetamine, one of the world's most addictive drugs.

"I was walking through the neighborhood, knocking on doors," he tells detectives. "It was real early, and I was surprised that no one was answering. I was about to give up and tried one more house, when someone finally answered."

That person was the older woman's boyfriend, Martin Shaw, a retiree in his late seventies. Shaw smiled at Dylan and said, "Can I help you?"

Dylan's response was to punch the older man in the face.

"He broke my hand," Dylan complains to detectives later, while being interviewed.

"How did he break your hand?"

"He had old teeth."

"I'm not following."

"I punched him in the face, and his old-man teeth broke my hand."

Blaming the injury on Shaw's teeth makes little sense, but people who abuse meth commonly develop psychotic episodes where they hallucinate and become increasingly paranoid.

Dylan flew into a rage. He forced his way inside and hit Shaw repeatedly. While the man lay on the floor, groaning and barely unconscious, Dylan darted into the kitchen, where he found a chef's knife. He then dragged Shaw down the hall to the bathroom and stabbed him to death.

Dylan has no memory of decapitating the man—or of taking off his belt and wrapping it around the throat and mouth of the severed head.

"Before you left the house," a detective says, "you turned on all the hot water. Why?"

Dylan shrugs.

A few streets away, Dr. Albert Bird was on the phone with a car mechanic when he turned to see a strange man covered in blood standing in his kitchen. The intruder was holding a severed head attached to a belt.

Dr. Bird screamed. He dropped the phone and tried to run.

The mechanic on the other end of the phone couldn't understand what was happening but heard Dr. Bird's agonized screams as he was being brutalized, so called 911.

Dylan takes a plea deal that spares him the death penalty. He's sentenced to two consecutive life terms.

A couple of years later, I'm visiting the dermatologist for my first skin checkup. I'm Irish, and after years of sunburns, I'm at risk for skin cancer.

The dermatologist is in his late thirties. As he begins

the exam, we get to talking. He asks me how I ended up going into law enforcement. I ask him how he became a doctor.

"I grew up on the wrong side of the tracks," he says. "My father was never in my life, and my mother was hardly around because she worked so much. But my best friend's dad was a doctor. I got interested in medicine because of him—wanted to *be* like him when I grew up. He took me under his wing. Later, when I was accepted into medical school, he paid my tuition."

"Wow."

"He did a lot of things like that, for a lot of people. I've never met anyone like him in my life. Just a tremendous person. A great soul. Then one day, out of nowhere, this maniac who was high on drugs broke into his house and butchered him to death."

I grow very still.

"The doctor," I say. "Where did he live?"

"Hollywood Hills."

"Are you talking about Dr. Albert Bird?"

The dermatologist's eyes light up. "Were you there? At the crime scene?"

"I helped with the investigation," I say, nodding. I tell him about the other victim, Martin Shaw.

"It seems Shaw was cut from the same cloth as Dr. Bird. He devoted his life to helping those in need. His real strength—what people I interviewed kept talking about—was how he mentored people of all ages on how to improve their lives, getting them jobs—you name it, he did it."

"That's . . . eerie."

"I know. This maniac happened to kill two men who, from all accounts, were exceptional, giving people."

"It's such a tragedy. Such a waste."

"I never knew either man," I say. "All I saw was how their lives got shattered. But until that moment, they touched so many lives—including mine. The way they lived showed me the type of person I want to be. The kind of cop who doesn't get cynical, always looks for the good in people."

ASHLEY SMITH

Two days after graduating college, Ashley Smith entered the police academy.

'm working a traffic detail when I spot a car with a red inspection sticker.

In our state, inspection stickers have a different color for every month of the year. Red is for December. It's now June. I pull the car over for an expired sticker.

The driver is a white male. His passenger is a Black female.

"You only pulled me over because I'm Black!" she screams.

"Ma'am, first of all, you're not driving. Second of all, you—"

"You guys hate us, and you kill us. It's all you people do. You're a piece of shit."

It's the second week in the trial of Derek Chauvin, the former Minneapolis police officer facing charges for the murder of

George Floyd. Hostility against cops is at an all-time high, the worst I've ever seen.

I let her vent. A quarter of my shift is traffic. The rest of the time, I'm handling calls. Normally, I thrive off chaos and difficult situations. My mind doesn't shut down. I'm able to control my emotions and act professionally. But I've pulled over fifteen cars today, and I'm so burned out, so sick of arguing politely with people. I want to go back to the station, to just sit and decompress. Write my traffic sheet and then go back out on patrol.

I look at the woman. I recognize her. I say, "Ma'am, do you remember me?"

"What?"

"Last summer, you were at a restaurant, eating at the bar and playing the Quick Draw lottery game with your friends."

She stares at me.

"Quick Draw lottery," I say. "All those screens around the bar, where you can either ask for a Quick Pick or choose ten of your own numbers and—"

"I know what it is."

"You asked for a playslip, wrote down your numbers, and ended up winning a hundred dollars. You handed the playslip to the bartender, and when you didn't get your money, she claimed you never handed her a ticket, and you claimed she stole your money."

"I don't remember you."

"Well, I remember you, because you called the police, and I was the one who responded to that call. The manager got involved, remember? He said that his bartender would never do such a thing, and I demanded he show me the security camera footage. It showed you did, in fact, hand in a playslip. It accidentally got misplaced, remember? I got you your money back. That case took six hours of my time."

"The only thing I remember is you treating me like shit."

The driver is looking at me, wide-eyed. He turns his head to his passenger, who I quickly learn is his girlfriend, and says, "Wait, hold on, Officer Smith here *was* the one who helped you. Why are you treating her like this?"

The boyfriend starts defending me, and eventually the woman apologizes. But right now, I'm so done with people treating me like crap. A good 95 percent of the people I've been dealing with over these past few weeks have been openly hostile, and it's exhausting. Frustrating.

I can see why cops become reclusive and turn to substance abuse. They don't want to be out in public because they've spent their entire week dealing with a nasty public.

That's why I'm a suicide prevention officer, part of a wellness program where officers can call and vent their frustrations. If they want, I can come to wherever they are, and we can sit and talk face-to-face. The program is 100 percent anonymous. It's helped remove the stigma of officers who ask for help.

Thank God I'm a part of this wellness program where I can offer positive, peer-on-peer support. Thank God I have the gym. It gets all those good endorphins going. I'll sacrifice sleep to hit the gym because missing it throws my attitude and energy off.

The community also offers opportunities to perform valuable acts of service.

I derive deep personal enjoyment and fulfillment from our department's "family day" events, where we help parents properly select and install child car seats, and host bicycle safety, assembly, and helmet-fitting lessons.

The biggest thrill for me is watching these young kids explore and play with our patrol cars, fire trucks, EMS vehicles, and our rescue helicopter. These kids haven't been soured by the world yet. They're excited to be with us and to talk to us.

I respond to a call where a young girl's bike is stolen. She's devastated. She had saved up her money to buy it. She swears, though her mother doesn't believe her, that when she took her bike to the grocery store she locked it up properly.

The detective and I decide to buy her a new bike, spending our own money. The mother isn't happy about it—wants to teach her a lesson about how to take care of her belongings—but seeing the way the girl's face lights up stays with me for weeks.

Moments like that bring me joy.

Moments like that keep me going.

PAUL WRIGHT

Paul Wright is a veteran of the City of Los Angeles Police Department.

I arrive at the apartment complex and see another police officer waiting for me, a guy with a good amount of experience. I'm here to investigate a family fight in progress, and he's my backup.

I'm twenty years old, a brand-spanking-new cop. We enter the building and cautiously start walking up the outside stairs. In the academy, we learned that, when it comes to domestic disturbance situations, police officers frequently get shot or injured.

I turn a corner and see a young woman a little older than me fleeing down the stairs, heading straight toward us. She's clearly in distress. Her face is puffy from crying, her eyes wet with tears.

My training kicks in. I immediately stop and do a threat assessment. *Does she present a danger? Do I need to have my hand on my gun—or am I overreacting?*

I look at her hands. She isn't holding a weapon. As I look behind her, to see if her husband or someone else is following, she wraps her arms around me and hugs me hard.

"Thank God you're here," she sobs, holding on to me for dear life. "Thank God you're here."

The stairwell is narrow, the steps steep. If the woman's husband comes running and decides to fight her, me, us, I'm going to be boxed in, which severely limits my options to defend myself and get the situation under control.

The problem is, this woman is so terrified she doesn't want to let go of me, let alone go back upstairs. My partner and I calm her down. We bring her downstairs.

"Wait right here," I say, and then my partner and I head up to her apartment. The husband is there with the couple's little girl.

The husband starts cursing us, calling me and my partner every name under the sun—right in front of his daughter. He's pissed that his wife called the police. He talks as though he's the victim here.

Then he turns to his daughter and says, "Honey, always remember that cops are bad people. They're assholes."

I grew up in a stable middle-class family. My parents loved and respected each other, and what I'm seeing right now is the complete opposite—and on top of that, this guy is justifying his actions.

I'm a twenty-year-old guy, unmarried, and I'm being asked to mitigate marital problems and domestic disputes. It's so foreign to me, I'm having a hard time processing it.

Shortly after this incident, I respond to another family disturbance call in a different apartment complex. This time, I'm the backup officer. When I arrive, another officer is already in the middle of dealing with a wife who is seething with rage. The husband, though, appears docile, and the officer is playing referee, trying to get the woman to calm down so he can get to the root of the issue.

The woman quickly grabs a cheese knife with a long blade, the kind with a prong for picking up cheese at the end. Before either of us can stop her, she stabs her husband deeply in his stomach.

After we subdue her, we call for medical aid for the husband.

I've always believed that God has a plan for everybody. A purpose. My own God-given talent—my purpose—I believe is to help people. I've wanted to be a cop since I was a young kid, back when I heard my best friend's dad, an LAPD detective sergeant who retired to Houston, Texas, tell stories about the job—and he had a *lot* of really cool stories.

I'm loving this job, the people I work with, the comradery we share. Each day is unpredictable, which I like, and there's plenty of action. But I've got to be careful. I don't want to become cynical, turn into someone who stops caring, because the moment that happens, I'm going to quit.

After a few more years of patrol, I become a detective. I'm assigned to the LAPD's South Bureau Homicide. It has sixty working detectives and four squads: the Seventy-Seventh,

Southeast, Harbor, and Southwest. I'm in the Southeast squad.

One year, we handle 428 murders. It's so bad in Los Angeles County that autopsies occur twenty-four hours a day, seven days a week. A lot of them are gang- and dope-related. The good news is that we have a 60 percent solve rate, which is especially impressive given that these gang-involved cases often hinge on uncooperative witnesses.

I'm working so much, and I'm so exhausted, that one day bleeds into the next. I don't have much time to think about the victims beyond making sure they get justice. No sooner do I finish one "callout"—getting a call at home to deal with a homicide—than I get another call to deal with a different homicide. We get so many murder calls, there are days when I never go home.

One Christmas Eve, the phone rings at midnight, waking me up from a sound sleep. There's been a homicide. I drive to the location, thinking, *This has got to be quick. I need to be with my kids.*

I've promised my kids I'd be there on Christmas morning, at my ex-wife's house, to watch them open their presents. I arrive at the crime scene, a single-story apartment at the top of a little hill. The uniform guys are out there, putting up the DO NOT CROSS banner tape.

Working as a police officer and a homicide detective, I've seen the saddest things in the world. I've been to other Christmas Eve crime scenes, when lonely people without family decide to kill themselves. I've seen the worst ways that people can treat other people. I've seen brains, blood, and carnage.

I check in with the officers, who put my name in the log and then give me a quick rundown of the crime. The victim is a big-time dope dealer—and a big guy. He weighs close to 350 pounds.

"He was celebrating with three prostitutes when a gang member decided it would be a good idea to rob him," the uniform says. "The body's in the apartment."

"Who called it in?"

"One of the prostitutes. She's in there, too."

The apartment is torn up. The victim is lying on the floor. He's been shot. There's lots of blood.

I talk to the prostitute. I've been told I have a way with people. All I do is treat them like human beings and make sure they're safe. She opens up and tells me what happened, says she didn't recognize the shooter.

"Did he make off with the dope?" I ask.

She shakes her head. "The two other girls took it and ran off."

No honor among thieves, I think. I get to work on the crime scene and manage to still make it to my ex-wife's house before the kids wake up.

I spend a lot of time working with the gang unit. One night my partner pulls up to a group of Grape Street Crip gang members who are sitting on a fence. These guys are well known to us.

I roll down the window. "What's up, fellas?"

They don't want to engage.

"Not here to jam you up," I say. "Just here to say hi, see what's going on."

I'm trying to keep it friendly but let them know we're in the area. A few of the guys come forward to say hello. My attention is locked on the remaining guy who stays sitting on the fence—a real skinny dude wearing an oversized T-shirt. He doesn't speak, and he refuses to make eye contact with us.

But it's his body language and the way he's watching the street that tells me something is seriously wrong. He's got an edge to him, and when he glances over at the patrol car, I see the look of someone itching for a fight.

I'm in the passenger seat. If this guy is armed and starts firing, I'm a sitting duck. I don't have any cover. I've got nowhere to hide.

I don't want to become paranoid, and I certainly don't want to believe everyone around me is bad. But in this job, I have to be vigilant. I have to be aware of safety, not only for myself, but also for my partner and the community.

We don't stay talking to the gang members for long. We need to respond to another call.

Half an hour later, another team from our gang unit responds to a robbery in progress at a residential home. The skinny guy who I thought was acting cagey and suspicious, I find out, pointed the gun at one of our officers. The officer fired and killed him.

I keep thinking about that moment when I was sitting in the car, watching this guy sitting on the fence only a few feet away. If he'd pulled his weapon then, he could've easily shot me in the head.

I've had friends who have been shot. I know a lot of officers who have been killed. So much of this job, I'm realizing, is about luck. When it's your time to go, it's your time to go, and there's not much you can do about it.

LAPD assigns me and nine other detectives to work with the FBI on a task force investigating gang members robbing banks. An informant tells me, "Hey, I just want you to know that there are some LA police officers involved in these bank robberies. They're hitting up the banks with the Rollin' 60s."

The Rollin' 60s are one of, if not *the*, most ruthless and violent gangs in the city.

"This is bullshit," I say. On the streets, I hear stories about crooked cops all the time. Gang members like to think we're all crooked. The truth is, the vast majority of us go at our job honestly. But dirty cops exist, and they're worse than the people we throw in jail.

With a huge smile, the informant gives me the details on a bank robbery involving these crooked cops.

My FBI partner and I pull the surveillance photos from the robbery. We blow one up and discover that one of the robbers is wearing a handheld radio clipped to his side. It has the shape of our police handheld radios, called rovers. I zoom in on the radio and, sure as shit, I can see LAPD stamped on it.

The bank robber is an LAPD cop.

My partner and I start an investigation. A handful of LAPD cops from one of the stations in South Bureau, we discover, have been involved in several of the bank robberies.

It doesn't end there.

These cops are also taking down dope houses with fictitious

search warrants. They show up wearing LAPD raid jackets and destroy houses, looking for drugs and cash.

Unfortunately for them, they also target the homes of people who aren't involved in the drug business. One person is an elderly woman. They tear through every inch of her home, slashing mattresses, everything. Fortunately for us, we have evidence and witnesses.

Our case is solid. Airtight. My partner and I present it to LAPD's Robbery-Homicide Division, and then we go to work with the people in Internal Affairs.

I can't believe this is happening.

I'm assigned a new task force to audit the Internal Affairs investigations of the officers involved. Each case brings me to the same conclusion. If their supervisors had done the proper follow-ups and asked even a couple of questions, all of this would have stopped much, much sooner.

When all the information has been properly vetted, the LAPD announces a press conference.

The scope of the corruption is enormous.

More than seventy officers are implicated in bank robberies, stealing drugs and selling them on the street. They planted evidence—and covered it up. They beat and shot people.

The ensuing scandal makes national headlines. Politicians and the media are quick to paint the entire LAPD with a broad brush, suggesting that the corruption is even more widespread than the public thinks. Community protestors fill the streets.

It's disheartening.

*   *   *

I'm called to a homicide in South Central LA. The banner tape is already up when I arrive. It's 4 a.m. and there's a party going on, literally, right next to the crime scene. People are having a barbecue, and there are kids running around.

Someone has been brutally murdered, and these people are carrying on like it's no big deal. What the hell?

I'm outside, examining the crime scene, when a young woman comes up to me and says, "Police don't care what happens to us people here."

Normally, I'd let a comment like that go. But lately I've been feeling frustrated about the antipolice sentiment, and this time I speak my mind.

"If I don't care, then why am I standing out here at four in the morning? Is it because I don't give a shit?"

She doesn't have anything to say about that.

My thoughts turn to my parents. I've been thinking about them a lot lately. Their whole lives, they worked their asses off and both died young. I don't want that to be me.

I've done this job for twenty-eight years. I've served the community to the best of my abilities. When I uncovered police corruption, I exposed it. I start thinking about friends of mine and acquaintances who were shot or killed in the line of duty. These officers gave their lives for this job, and now, everywhere I turn, all I hear about is how awful and corrupt the police are. How we don't care.

Well, I do care. But it's becoming harder not to turn into the cynical person I always told myself I wouldn't be. I don't want to stop caring, because the moment I do, it will be time for me to go.

MITCHELL WIDO

Mitchell Wido is a veteran of the Bureau of Alcohol, Tobacco, Firearms and Explosives (ATF).

'm detailed out to a team covering the Illinois State Police narcotics task force.

Today, Theodore Young, a special agent with the state police, is working undercover, about to meet with two suspects. In what's called a reverse, Young is going to portray a narcotics dealer and sell them two kilos of coke for $40,000.

To legally monitor conversations, the State of Illinois requires a court "overhear" order. But securing a court order takes time and most drug deals, like this one, are only set up an hour or so before they happen.

A second state requirement is two-party consent. That means Young can't wear a wire.

But I'm federal, a special agent with the Bureau of Alcohol, Tobacco, Firearms and Explosives, and federal law allows one-party consent—which means I can legally have Young wear a wire. I want him to wear one in case he gets into trouble, so I give him a wire to insert into his belt. The thing is, I'm the only cover team agent that has an ATF radio that's set to monitor the wire. I will be the only one able to hear it.

Young is also given a panic button, a silent transmitter that emits a tone over the radio to alert the cover team when it's time to move in and effect the arrest. He places it in the pocket of his jeans.

It's 11 a.m. when I drive to the South Side of Chicago and park in a driveway around the corner from the deal site, a gas station.

The homes in this neighborhood are packed together tightly. The sidewalk directly in front of me leads to a street partially blocked by a big evergreen tree. Behind that is a gangway that leads straight to the gas station.

I've got a good view of the gas pumps, but I can't see Young—our U/C, or undercover cop. I can't see the suspects, either, but I can hear their voices over Young's wire.

"Let's see the money," Young says, kicking off the negotiations.

This is how it always goes. You show me yours and I'll show you mine and then we'll do the deal. Dope-dealer etiquette dictates that the money is always displayed first.

Our plan is that as soon as they show the money, the buyers are going down.

"No problem," a suspect says. "Got the money in my car. It's parked just around the corner."

Around the corner?

Moving a deal that's already in process—that's not supposed to happen. Are these two suspects setting Young up for a rip-off?

My thoughts shift to his cover team. Right now, Young's guys are locked into certain positions so they can watch him and move in quickly to effect the arrest. Everything was perfectly choreographed for the gas station. A sudden location change can throw the whole operation into chaos.

Young is a big guy, very intimidating, and a smooth talker. A pro. Over the wire, he says, "I'll get in my car and follow you."

To where? Young was told about the meeting spot at the last minute. We have no idea where the suspects are parked.

Voices from his cover team come over the radio.

"Where is he going?"

"I can't see him."

"We don't have eyes on the U/C."

The big evergreen blocks my view of the side street, but I see a flash of two people walking by. Could be the suspects, could be someone else. A moment later, I see a car. It's Young's car, I'm sure of it. I can make out the Cadillac's back bumper.

My windows are halfway down, and I hear a car door open. I get ready. *The moment Young hits the panic button, I'll leave the car and approach on foot. Until then, I'll stay put, advise the cover team members where they're at, and monitor the wire for—*

"Don't shoot."

Young's voice. It's jumped about twenty octaves.

"Take whatever you—"

I exit my car and draw my SIG Sauer 9mm.

"Please, don't shoot."

Leaving the radio behind, I can now hear Young's voice directly. He's pleading for his life.

I quickly approach the evergreen, using it for cover. The moment I make my way around the tree, it's going to be a shitstorm.

I pause for a moment, then round the tree and see Young on his knees, his hands in the air. *He didn't have time to reach into his jean pocket and trigger the panic button,* I think, my attention swinging to the offender holding a gun to the back of Young's head. A second offender, his back to me, holds a chrome revolver. It's pointed at Young's face.

"Police!" I yell, knowing what's going to happen next.

The offenders are standing twenty feet away; their eyes—and guns—shift to me.

They start firing, *pop-pop-pop-pop-pop.*

I return fire. The gunfight lasts seconds. I manage to wound the two shooters.

The cover team arrives as I'm checking myself for gunshots. I don't have a scratch on me.

The suspects are arrested.

Young is fine. He tells us he'd felt comfortable relocating the deal because he thought—mistakenly—that his cover team was right behind him.

At first, we figured Young's cover had been blown. It wasn't. The two men, we discover, thought Young was a legitimate dope dealer. Their plan was to rip him off, possibly even kill him.

Later that night, I'm at home with my family, mentally

replaying the shooting and thinking about how lucky I am to be alive, when an ATF peer support counselor calls me. He's been told about the shooting.

"How are you doing?" he asks.

Showing emotion is a sign of weakness. Suck it up and carry on. That's my mantra.

"I'm fine," I tell him.

"I'm told you guys exchanged sixteen gunshots. It's amazing you didn't get hit."

It *is* amazing. A miracle, when I stop and think about it.

He asks how my family is doing. I tell him everything's great, and then he starts describing the warning signs of post-traumatic stress. He's doing his job, I get that, but I don't want to hear this touchy-feely stuff. When he gets into the effects of PTSD, I stop him short.

"I'm doing A-OK, honest," I say politely. "Now, if Young was hurt or killed, or if one of my rounds hit an innocent person, well, then I probably would need to talk. Fortunately, only the bad guys got shot, and I'm totally fine with how everything turned out. It's all good."

Six months later, I get a call out of the blue from HQ asking if I want to be a peer support critical incident counselor. Mental health has become a critical area in law enforcement, and Bill Hogwood, a former cop and a pioneer PTSD effects officer, is leading a new support unit.

I'm not sure why I'm being asked, aside from the fact that I was involved in a shooting. I don't think I'll be any good at this, but I agree to do it, and go for training just outside of DC. The immersive coursework helps me realize that I know nothing about PTSD—how pervasive it is, how it can sneak up on you. I also realize why I closed off emotionally right after the shooting.

My father lost his mother when he was a young kid and was raised by his father, who worked long hours. At seventeen, my father went into the Army and was a paratrooper in World War II. He never showed any emotion when a relative died, even when my mother was sick in the hospital. I followed his example. I was young and didn't know any better. Looking back, I realize my father was battling his own demons.

My philosophy has always been to help where needed. If I could help a fellow agent or police officer—or even family members or coworkers—deal with trauma, I was all for it. Now I'm better equipped to really make a difference.

Not too long after my training, I start going out on peer support responses, talking to other agents who have gone through critical incidents. I don't try to make them talk if they don't want to, nor do I try to coax out their feelings. But just like I was trained, I do my best to educate them on the warning signs of PTSD. I emphasize that if they need to talk, they should talk—because a whole lot of people, like me, have gone through similar traumatic incidents and can understand their feelings. I let them know I'm not an expert or a psychologist, just a fellow agent and peer who cares and wants to help.

Some agents respond to their situations the same way I did. *Everything's fine, no problems here, just let me get back to work.* For some people, that's even true. Others aren't as lucky. When it comes to PTSD, dark thoughts can sneak up on the best, most veteran officers when they least expect it.

*   *   *

Years later, I'm in St. Louis attending our annual peer support training conference, when we get word of a school shooting in Columbine, Colorado. The class stops and everyone gathers in front of TVs to watch the news unfold live.

The police have cordoned off the school. There's no information about the offender. We don't know if it's a single shooter or shooters, or if they've been apprehended, fled the scene, or are still inside the school targeting students. We watch as some students file out with hands above their heads, passing bodies covered by blood-soaked sheets. Wounded students fall out of windows. Trapped students hold hand-drawn signs at windows, asking for medical help.

What I'm witnessing...it's unprecedented. Our country has never seen or experienced anything like this. And none of us for a single moment imagine that in the years to follow, incidents like Columbine will become disgustingly common.

Within minutes, Bill Hogwood, the ATF's peer support team coordinator, gets a call from Washington. Several ATF agents from the Denver Field Division have responded to the scene at Columbine. They're dealing with a lot of death and carnage as they investigate the recovered firearms and explosives. Washington wants Peer Support out there ASAP. I arrive with the team, three counselors, and a chaplain the next day.

Normally, we would wait until the initial event is over to designate an office or even a hotel meeting room to triage support. Given the scope of this unprecedented traumatic event, Hogwood and our bosses decide that the team will go to the scene of the ongoing investigation so that any first responder knows he or she has support.

That evening, we finish setting up a staging area in a back parking lot at the high school. More than thirty hours have passed since the critical event. But because of the enormous amount of evidence that needs to be documented, the bodies of the deceased victims are still inside the school. The shooters detonated numerous IEDs, some of which are still live and inside the school, on the property, and in vehicles.

Before the bodies can be moved, the crime scene needs to be searched, documented, and processed; and any remaining IEDs need to be located, rendered safe, removed, and disposed of.

And until the medical examiner makes a positive identification, nothing official can be told to the parents.

We're approached by a few officers and other first responders. I can see the grief and torment on their faces. They thank us for being here, and then head into the school because they have jobs to do. They'll deal with their emotions later. I hope they'll reach out to someone later, when they can.

I'm approached by an investigator. "A Jefferson County bomb technician asked me to locate an ATF guy, to see if you have a CES on-scene."

"I'm a certified explosives specialist," I say. "I'll talk to him."

I follow the investigator into the school and walk past hundreds of bullet holes, each one marked with a yellow Post-it note. The hallway is a sea of small yellow squares.

I pass numerous "blast seats"—locations where explosive

devices have gone off—and see the metal fragmentation of pipe bombs and the charred remains of Molotov cocktails.

The classrooms are eerily empty. Books and backpacks scattered across the floor, desks overturned. One floor is covered in a pool of dried blood. I see a pair of glasses, a family photograph, and a posterboard that says 1 BLEEDING TO DEATH.

I remember seeing that sign on TV. It's one that students held out the windows, for the police.

The body of one victim lies on the stairwell. Another is just outside the library.

I enter the room. This is where the shooters, now ID'd as fellow high school students Dylan Klebold and Eric Harris, gunned down the last of their victims before turning their weapons on themselves.

More of their victims are here. On the floor, under desks, in their chairs.

I'm a parent of a school-aged child. I think of the victims, their families.

I'll deal with my feelings later. Right now, I have a job to do.

The bomb techs working the library advise me that they can see several live devices still in the pockets of the shooters: CO_2 cartridges with wicks made of matchsticks. These IEDs are miniature pipe bombs that fragment and can cause serious wounds or death. The shooters added additional shrapnel by gluing BBs around the bombs.

The shooters also took match strikers and fashioned them into makeshift bracelets taped to their wrists. I know why they did this. It was so that they could continue shooting with one hand while the other reached into a pocket, grabbed a bomb, struck the matchstick wick against the striker board, and then threw it like a grenade.

The bomb tech wants to know the best way to go about collecting these live devices. My suggestion is to cut the clothing from the shooters, then safely collect each IED individually.

When we're finished, we find twenty-six unexploded devices inside the library. More are being discovered inside the cafeteria, hallways, and classrooms.

Once all the devices are recovered from the area, EMTs arrive with body bags to finally remove the deceased from the library.

It's the second day after the shooting, and none of these victims have been formally identified yet. Their parents sent these kids off to school, thinking it was just another ordinary day. Now their families... a part of them is clinging to the hope, however unlikely, that their missing sons and daughters might be alive and hiding somewhere, while another part is preparing for the fact that their children are dead.

These families, they're going through hell. The thought won't leave my mind. I repeatedly shake my head to keep my mind straight. *Gotta stay in work mode.*

I help place several of the students in body bags and help carry them to a staging area where ambulances will transport them to the medical examiner's office.

As I wait for their arrival, I stare down a long row of black zippered bags, each holding someone's kid. Out of respect for the families, we've placed the bodies of the two shooters, Klebold and Harris, on the other side of the staging area, away from where we've gathered their victims.

This small act is something we can do for the victims' families even if they never know that we did it. That and saying prayers over their dead children.

The chaplain says a prayer over each of the victims. Someone asks if he's going to do the same for the shooters.

"No," the chaplain says. "God can say prayers for those two if He wants. I'm not going to do it."

The ambulances are inbound. We can fit three bodies inside each one.

When the body bags are loaded, we're down to one last ambulance and three remaining bodies: the shooters and one of their victims. We don't know who. Could be a boy or a girl. All we know is that lying inside that body bag is the son or daughter of a family hoping beyond hope for a call that their child has been found safe and is coming home.

Hogwood speaks up and addresses the group. "The shooters are going in their own ambulance. I'm not going to disrespect these families by putting their son or daughter inside an ambulance with the person who killed them."

Hogwood demands that another ambulance be sent to transport the last victim alone. We stay with that lone student until the last ambulance arrives.

Many years later—I don't remember the exact date—I'm sitting at home, flipping through the TV channels. It's the middle of the night and I can't sleep.

I'm thinking about Iraq.

I've just returned from my second tour, as part of a Department of Defense task force that helped investigate roadside bombs. I'd also gone there previously with a State Department mission, instructing the Iraqi police on how to conduct postblast investigations. I return to the States, haunted by a memory of a soldier's helmet sticking out from an empty body bag. His name printed on the desert camo cover. I obsessively hunt down who the soldier is, relieved when I find out he survived and is doing okay.

But there were numerous other occasions where the outcome wasn't positive. At the time, I had to stay focused on the job.

On the TV, I stumble on a scene from what appears to be a made-for-TV movie where an upper-middle-class family—a mother and father and their teenage daughter—are sitting in the kitchen, talking about their eldest daughter, who is missing.

Probably just ran away from home, I think.

As I watch the scene unfold, I quickly realize that this family is waiting for a phone call from a detective. Their eldest daughter is a student at Columbine High School.

For a reason I can't explain, I suddenly feel extremely guilty for assuming the girl was just a runaway. My feelings of guilt build and my mind spins back to my time inside the library, where I stood next to the victims who were inside the school for thirty hours, waiting to be identified.

Then I see the hallway, a sea of yellow Post-it notes.

Those CO_2 IEDs I found inside the shooters' pockets.

I'm now in the grip of an emotional hurricane. I can't stop it. I can only brace myself.

A phone rings in the TV movie. The father answers the

phone. The detective on the other end of the line asks if their daughter has a tattoo.

"No," the father says, visibly relieved. "My daughter doesn't have a tattoo."

The youngest daughter sitting at the kitchen table says her older sister does, in fact, have a tattoo. The parents look at her with disbelief.

The sister's eyes fill with tears. "She made me promise not to tell you."

"What kind of tattoo?" the father asks, his voice hollow. "Where?"

She tells him, and the father relays the information to the detective. It's the same tattoo as one of the female Columbine victims.

This victim has been positively identified. Their daughter will not be coming home.

As the family breaks down in grief, I'm still tossed inside the eye of the hurricane, gripped by flashbacks from both Columbine and Iraq.

One flashback: It's early morning and I'm dressed in body armor, riding a bus to conduct training at an Iraqi police station. The bus comes to a sudden stop. We've received intel that the Iraqi police are about to be attacked. Instead of training, we're shipped home. I'm told that the station and the police officers were blown up.

I'm investigating roadside bombs. The situations are high-pressure. We've got to process the scenes quickly, no more than fifteen minutes, because we could be attacked at any moment.

The hurricane lasts seconds. It spits me back out and then

vanishes. The sky is clear, yet I feel like I've been knocked on my ass.

I don't know what to do, but I know what I need to do.

I need to get up and get ready for work.

I need to do my job.

I need to help people. That's my mission.

MIKE SOLAN

Mike Solan works in the Pacific Northwest.

The wife is really scared.

I am, too. Cops who say they're not afraid aren't being honest. You have to be afraid—have to respect your fear or you'll end up being careless and reckless.

I've arrived at the scene of a domestic violence call. I'm standing outside the house with the husband. The husband is a very large fellow.

I always look at the person I'm dealing with as someone who can annihilate me. As long as I have that healthy respect, I feel that I can turn my fear into an advantage.

The level of hostility and abuse this man has for his wife is now being directed at me—not physically (at least not yet), but he's trying to control me verbally. The guy is in my face, just inches away, screaming in such rage he's spitting on me.

I don't take it personally. His anger isn't being directed at me but at the uniform, the moral high ground I represent. I've learned not to let my emotions take over my thought process in a negative way. It's the only way to be an effective cop.

I'm not the biggest guy, but I'm athletic and pretty fast and I know how to wrestle. I'm confident in my abilities. I also need a partner who can help me.

My partner knows we have to take this guy into custody— knows that the moment I put my hands on him, the husband is going to put up a fight. My partner just stands there, unsure of what to do, maybe not knowing what he should do.

In every situation, you've got to have a plan. You've got to limit how you'll go hands-on with somebody so you don't get hurt, which means you have to think through things, look for opportunities to help solve the problem.

Behind the husband, a few feet away, I spot a small barbecue.

I step forward. The guy steps back, but he doesn't let up on his verbal attack.

I take another step, then another, and as I keep walking, the guy keeps moving backward, screaming at me. He walks into the barbecue and falls ass over teakettle.

I go hands-on with him. My partner wakes up and gets involved. The two of us get into a little bit of a struggle with the husband, but we're able to get him into custody.

Later that night, I'm in a different neighborhood and walking back to my patrol car when a cat comes up to me. I reach down and start petting it and notice it has a tag. The address on it belongs to a different neighborhood.

I pick up the cat, drive it to the address, and knock on the door. It's late, so it takes a while for someone to answer.

A woman answers the door. The cat bolts from my arms and runs inside the house.

The woman bursts into tears.

"Thank you," she says. "Thank you so much. We've been trying to find our cat for months."

The woman and her family are so appreciative they write a letter of commendation, thanking me. It's a small gesture, but that humanity, seeing people who respect life, has a deep impact on me.

The good majority of individuals I come into contact with on a nightly basis don't have any concern for their actions. They're going to do what they want to do. They don't care for others, only themselves. I think back to a violent gangbanger I dealt with on multiple occasions. He was shot ten times, and I was the first to arrive on the scene.

This gangbanger had zero regard for other people. When I approached him, he looked up at me, panic-stricken, and said, "Help me."

Then he died.

What I always remember—what I always carry with me—is that, at the end of the day, this violent person who didn't care for anyone but himself was terrified and asked me for help.

People expect cops to serve. I serve people who appreciate us and people who hate us. When you're a cop, you can't be biased in your service. You have to serve everybody.

PART THREE:

Defend

JOHN BOWMAN

John Bowman is a special agent for the Bureau of Alcohol,
Tobacco, Firearms and Explosives (ATF).

Billy Baxter's name on the streets is BB because he can run
fast as a bullet. He's wanted on federal charges for moving weapons across state lines and also on municipal charges
relating to gun crimes. BB is also wanted for multiple shootings in the city where he lives and is an active member of a
gang that pushes large quantities of drugs.

Going after a main drug supplier is the job of the DEA.
The ATF focuses on violent crime associated with drugs. We
work with the local police.

Eight of us, divided into two teams, are surveilling the
area around the duplex where BB lives, waiting for him to
pop up.

One of the teams of two comes over the radio and says, "BB is out of the house. Everybody, move into position."

We're given BB's location. My partner, Dale Williams, a police officer, is behind the wheel. He pulls out of our spot and takes off.

Seconds later, someone on the radio says, "He's taking off, he's running, he's running."

Everyone hits their sirens.

The chase is on.

I'm not surprised BB is running. When guys get on the radar of the ATF or FBI, they're looking at ten-, twenty-, thirty-year sentences or, sometimes, life sentences.

We arrive at a corner, and I see BB, this small guy, thin and lithe, dressed in baggy basketball shorts, an NBA jersey, a baseball hat, and high-tops. He's moving fast, running for his life.

Williams gets close and hits the brakes. As we get out to pursue on foot, I hear a voice on the radio shout, *"Gun, he's got a gun!"*

I'm young—twenty-seven—and in good shape. I've recently graduated from the academy, and I've only been on the job for a few weeks. Williams is in his late fifties, and much heavier. He can't keep up.

"Get him," he says to me, between huffing and puffing. "You're on your own."

I'm chasing after BB, thinking, *Oh, God, does this guy still have the gun? Should I draw?*

If I pull my weapon, I'm going to have to slow down to remove it from the holster. And I really want to catch this guy.

But if I don't have my gun out and BB turns and starts shooting at me, then I'm an idiot.

I yell "Police!" but BB doesn't stop. I'm starting to gain on him, the sirens growing louder, and I'm wondering if I should push him or just tackle him when we hit an intersection.

BB runs across it. I'm closing the gap.

A car skids onto the curb in front of me. My boss is behind the wheel—and he's about to hit me. I jump over the hood, avoiding impact, and continue chasing after our guy.

BB has managed to get a little ahead of me, but I'm close enough to see him run into a house. I call it in over the radio.

Moments later, we have the house surrounded. He gets up on the roof to try to escape. One of our guys spots him, and BB ducks back inside the house.

Now he's barricaded.

SWAT shows up, and after some tense negotiation, BB agrees to come out.

It's my first arrest.

The morning before Valentine's weekend, I'm driving to work when I get a call from my training agent.

"Where are you?" he asks.

"I'm on my way in."

"There's been a shooting outside an elementary school. Police want our help."

He gives me an address on the north side of the city, an area well known for street-gang activity.

I arrive at the scene and find out what happened.

Early this morning, two gangs spotted each other and

unleashed about a hundred shots, right in front of the school. Now an eleven-year-old girl is dead. It's a complete miracle more kids weren't killed.

The case is all over the papers and news. One paper prints a picture of the crime scene below the headline "Shame on This City." Seeing the grief of the family and friends tears me apart, emboldens me and everyone else working this case to work as hard as humanly possible. I keep the faces of the victim's family in my mind and get to work with other ATF agents to identify some of the players, find out where they lived.

One of our old informants calls us. He's so distraught about what happened at the school he gives the names of the two gangs involved.

We provide that information to the police. Working together, we find three gang members who were there the morning of the shooting. All three are felons with open cases involving guns, but we don't have any way of proving they had anything to do with the actual murder of the eleven-year-old girl.

We come up with the idea of charging them for their open gun cases. It will take them off the streets and, hopefully, we can get them to talk. The city police agree with our plan.

Now we've got to find these three guys.

We work the entire Valentine's Day weekend and grab two pretty quickly.

The two gang members won't talk. At first. When forced to deal with the ATF or FBI, there are those who tell and those who wish they did.

Then the reality that they're dealing with federal charges dawns on them, and while they don't exactly give up the shooter, they give us enough information to point to the fact that the third gang member we're looking for is the one who killed the eight-year-old girl.

His name is Mark Robinson. He has an extensive criminal history.

We work out leads and get information that Robinson could be in one of two houses. We hit them early in the morning and come up empty.

Another informant tells us our guy is in a flophouse, the kind where drug users go to shoot up and get high. We hit it.

Robinson isn't there. We interview the users.

"Yeah, I know him," one tells us. "He's got himself a new girlfriend. Mandy something. She's trying to help him get out of town."

Mandy, we find out after extensive investigative research, is Mandy Garcia. We have her home and work address, the kind of car she drives—we know everything about her. On Saturday night, we drive out to the place where she works and surveil the building.

Mandy shows up in her car.

There's a male sitting in the passenger seat.

Oh, my God, I think, *this could be him.*

It's not. The male passenger is her brother.

We interview her. She tells us where she believes Robinson is. We quickly rally and assemble a team to hit Robinson's house later that night.

And, sure as shit, there he is. We arrest him and help the police with the charges for all the players involved.

In a bin on my desk, I collect news articles, court documents, impact statements from victims. It's mind-blowing what they and their families go through. I open the young girl's file, read the words of her family, then look down at my desk in silence.

I don't talk about work when I'm at home. I completely shut down. I need that separation, but I don't always get it. There are reports to read and affidavits to write—and the phone never stops ringing.

Tonight, I'm meeting my wife for dinner. We haven't spent any time alone in weeks.

As soon as we arrive at the restaurant, my phone rings. She tries to hide her frustration as I check caller ID.

It's one of my informants. This person has crucial information on a very big case.

She sees the look on my face, knows that dinner is canceled. Again.

"I'm sorry," I tell her. "But I've got to take this call."

PATRICK DUGAN

Patrick Dugan's father, grandfather, and great-grandfather, as well as his uncle and a cousin, were police officers. He joined the Air Force after graduating from college. Nine years later, at thirty-two, he entered the FBI Academy.

Graduation day is a huge event.

Like everyone else, I'm dressed in my J. Edgar Hoover suit, black wingtip shoes, white shirt, and conservative tie. After enduring four and a half months of training, it's an emotional moment for me—for all of us. As we're being sworn in, the guy next to me, a tough-as-nails Marine, has tears in his eyes.

I know how he feels. The pride in wearing the badge. The tremendous responsibility we've been given.

After the ceremony, we get wheeled off to the armory,

where we're issued our SIG Sauers. Then we're taken to the break room, given a glass of punch, and told, "Go out and do good things."

The FBI's mission is to protect the citizens of the United States. We investigate everything from counterterrorism, counterintelligence, and cybercrimes to white-collar crime, public corruption, and gangs. I'm sent to the Baltimore field office, where I'll be working in their Violent Crimes/Major Offenders Squad with a focus on bank robberies.

On my first day, I check in at 7:30 a.m. It's a Monday. A couple of minutes after nine, my field training agent walks over to my desk and says, "We got a bank holdup. Let's go."

I'm brand-spanking-new, no idea what I'm supposed to do when we get to the bank.

My field training agent and the agents working the crime scene have decades of law enforcement experience. One, a guy named O'Sullivan, comes up to me and says, "Your job is to sit in my back pocket until I tell you otherwise. I don't want you to say or do anything stupid."

I keep my mouth shut and my ears open.

O'Sullivan interviews the bank teller—a young mother. "He walked in by himself and passed me a note. It said, 'This is a holdup, give me all your money.' And I did."

"Did he have a weapon?"

"I didn't see one."

She touches her hand to her throat, as if imagining all the ways her encounter could have gone. If he was armed, she could have been injured or, worse, killed.

Later, when I'm alone with O'Sullivan, he says, "Everything here points to a lone offender. Guys who pass notes, they've generally done this before, have a long rap sheet. They're smart enough to know that if they don't show a weapon, they'll face a shorter jail sentence."

For a rookie FBI agent, it's a pretty exciting first day.

I keep thinking about the bank teller. She woke up this morning wanting to go to work, do a good job, and go home to her family. She ended the day terrified that the offender might rob the bank again, maybe figure out that she talked to the FBI and follow her home. She'll remain in a constant state of fear unless we can bring her closure.

Fortunately, we do.

Robberies don't happen by accident. Whether offenders are working alone or in groups, they're following a conscious decision-making process. Go into a business and forcefully demand cash.

Bank robbers tend to have a certain "style"—wearing the same clothes and masks, hitting banks a certain way. Even if they're arrested and go to prison, upon release they usually revert back to their practiced habits.

It's not hyperbole. These offenders look at robbing banks as a job they do in between jail time. And, interestingly, it's a job that's frequently passed from generation to generation. One guy I recently locked up for bank robbery was the thirty-year-old son of an incarcerated bank robber.

Three years later, I have more than a hundred bank robbery cases under my belt. I get a nighttime call from a cop in Baltimore County.

"Found a guy dumped in a field. He's the assistant manager of a credit union. Says he entered his apartment complex parking lot a little after 6 p.m. and was kidnapped by three masked people and held at gunpoint."

The FBI always partners with detectives in these cases. We interview the victim, a former Marine. He hasn't been beaten up but was manhandled pretty good, and he's clearly shaken as he walks us through what happened.

"The kidnappers pepper-sprayed me, then placed me on the car's floorboard. I think it was a black four-door sedan. They held a shotgun to my head. They drove me to the bank where I work and forced me to hand over the keys and the alarm code."

He takes a deep drink from a glass of water. "When they came back, from what I could hear they managed to gain entry but were pissed because the money was more secured than they anticipated." He swallows, his eyes steady. "I was sure they were going to kill me."

The offenders, I find out the next day, did, in fact, leave with a significant amount of cash—but not as much as they were hoping to score. Witnesses at the scene report seeing a similar black four-door sedan near the bank on the day of the robbery, four people inside.

Over the next couple of months, twelve more robberies go down all over the state. Although the group mixes up what they wear, and the time of day they hit, most of the cases include an armed carjacking and some violence against bank employees. The same suspicious black four-door sedan is spotted casing a bank days before it's robbed.

There are dozens of victims—dozens of people who had a gun waved in their faces and were told to get down on the floor or their brains would be blown out. The violence and fear they've endured is on our minds as the FBI works these cases with detectives across multiple police departments. Every member of the investigative team is tremendously smart and dedicated, working day in and day out to help bring justice for the victims.

I'm in my office, sifting through lists of possible offenders, when I get a call about another bank robbery. "It's the same crew," a detective tells me, "but this time they left us a gift."

I arrive at the bank. Witnesses tell us one of the masked men rushed across the lobby and racked the slide of a nine-millimeter handgun to announce and emphasize his presence with authority.

The "gift" is an ejected round.

It's our first piece of physical evidence.

Then we get lucky.

A woman calls 911. "My boyfriend assaulted me."

The Baltimore police respond to the domestic violence call. A black four-door sedan is seen driving away just as patrol arrives. The police are aware that a similar vehicle has been used in a string of bank robberies.

"Was that your vehicle that just drove away?" they ask her.

"No. It belongs to my boyfriend. His name is Brad Young. You know all those bank robberies that've taken place over the last couple of months? He's the ringleader."

"Why are you telling us about him now?"

"Because he didn't give me my cut from our last job," she replies. "We got into a big fight, and he beat me up."

The police go after the car. A brief chase ensues. Young ends up crashing his car but manages to get away before the police catch up to him.

Inside the sedan's trunk is a boatload of cash, some of which is stained from a dye pack. A dye pack is a radio-controlled security device set to a timer. It's fitted inside a stack of money, and typically activates within seconds of the cash leaving a bank. In addition to producing a reddish-orange dye that stains clothes and skin, a dye pack also emits tear gas and a chemical compound that reduces the money to ash. (I once investigated a robbery where an offender put an activated dye pack down the front of his pants—and ended up in the ER with burns on his genitals.)

The Baltimore police also find a nine-millimeter handgun in the car. We send it to the lab, where scientists compare the tool markings on the ejected round to the recovered handgun's extractor.

It's a perfect match.

Everything flows from there.

The girlfriend who called the police agrees to cooperate with the government in exchange for a reduced sentence. Her name is Karen. She shares a lot of interesting information with us.

For the past twenty years, she's been working as an administrator for a large government agency in DC. A friend introduced her to Brad Young before he went to prison for a previous crime. They kept in touch while he was incarcerated, and when he was released, he decided he was going to start robbing banks, and she agreed to help case locations for him. She also acted as the getaway driver in several of the robberies.

The group, Karen tells us, is comprised of five men: Young and four others. One of the other offenders has a girlfriend named Sandy, who works as a bank teller.

"Sandy set up her coworkers and her branch for one of the robberies," Karen says.

Police pick up Sandy while my group focuses on Young, the ringleader. He's still on the run. The FBI puts out arrest warrants for Young and the others.

Then I get a call from police in Richmond, Virginia.

"There was a car accident on Interstate 95," the officer tells me. "We ran the names of two males through our system and found out you guys have arrest warrants on them. We've got them in custody."

"Which ones?" I ask.

It's Brad Young and the guy who served as wheelman in most of the robberies.

Two of the five offenders have now been caught.

I get to work trying to locate the guy who held the shotgun against the former Marine's head during the first carjacking. My squad and I track him down in Baltimore County and arrest him.

The fourth member of the group is arrested for shoplifting steaks from a grocery store in Florida. When the police run his name, they see his federal arrest warrant and call us.

The last man—the one who looked out for the police while the others were robbing the bank—is hard to locate. We know his name, but we don't have any booking photos of him because he's never been arrested.

We finally track him down through an informant.

When we arrive at his house, the suspect answers the door with his hands up.

"You've got me," he says.

In the FBI, we call that a clue.

*   *   *

A lone man carrying a gun walks into a bank and robs it. Because he wears gloves and a mask, we don't recover any fingerprints, and the security footage isn't helpful. All we have is a general physical description.

He repeats the same pattern in eight more robberies, all at banks in the I-695 Baltimore Beltway area.

The robber is meticulous. Judging from our investigation, it appears he isn't using a wheelman or a lookout.

We have very good working relationships with bank security officers in the area. An officer from a major national bank calls me and says, "Hey, I don't know if this is of any interest to you, but a customer at our Essex branch turned in a dye-stained $20 bill."

Essex is the east side of Baltimore County. I drive to the bank and talk to the branch manager.

"Do you know who turned in the $20 bill?"

The branch manager nods. "She's a regular customer of ours. She came in with some cash the other day, handed me the dye-stained twenty and said, 'I don't know what to do with this.'"

The manager gives me the woman's address, and I drive out to her house. She's a single mother in her midthirties. Pleasant and cooperative.

"My eight-year-old daughter found that $20 bill in our driveway," she tells me. "This was a few days ago."

"Anyone on your property that day?"

"Just my tenant. Well, my former tenant. That was the day he moved out."

She gives me his name—Lee White—and a little information on him, including what kind of pickup truck he drives.

That's all she knows, but it's a good start. I go back to the office and plug the information into our internal computer system, which keeps detailed records of bank robberies all over the country.

The computer lights up like a pinball machine. Lee White has been involved in a lot of prior crimes and in the past has been convicted at least twice of armed bank robbery. He also has a demonstrated violent streak.

After running White through the computer system, I seek out the case agent. "I covered this lead today. Seemed like it might not go anywhere at first, but I think this guy looks good for your series of bank robberies in the I-695 Baltimore Beltway area."

I show her the computer printouts on White. "I don't know where he's currently living, but this guy has already hit nine banks. There's a good chance he's going to stick to the Beltway when he hits the next one. He's not going to stop—and he's getting more violent."

The case agent is excited and runs with it.

What happens next would never be believable in a movie or TV show, but it happens in real life.

We start surveilling banks in the Beltway area, our only information a description of White's pickup truck. At two in the afternoon one day, it's spotted in a gas station parking lot near a Porsche dealership right up the street from a bank.

The man sitting in the truck is a perfect match for the booking photos we have of Lee White.

We believe White's our bank robber, but since we don't

have any proof that would be usable in court, we coordinate a surveillance operation. But as FBI agents and police officers watch from their unmarked cars, the Porsche dealership catches on fire.

Is White behind it? Did he set the fire to create a diversion?

We watch him, waiting for him to leave his car, but he just sits there, waiting.

It's a major, four-alarm fire. The fire and police departments come in and shut down three blocks south of the dealership and three blocks north. No one can get in or out of the area.

Our suspect continues to sit in the truck.

It takes hours to put out the fire. At 7 p.m., the roads are reopened. By then, all the banks are closed for the day. It doesn't seem that White had anything to do with the fire—it was just a strange coincidence. He starts his truck and drives away.

We follow. Now we know where he's living.

The next day, our suspect jumps into his truck and drives to the exact same parking lot right up the street from the bank. We're sure he's going to hit the bank today.

Being out in the field and working a real-world op is an adrenaline rush. We're setting up our surveillance, moving agents and officers into key positions, when the suspect takes off.

We lose him momentarily, then find his truck parked in a different area.

White's not in it.

Where could he have gone? We only lost sight of him for about a minute. He must be somewhere nearby—

A detective speaks on the radio. "Got a bank robbery in process. It's right down the street."

Did he hurt anyone? Did he, God forbid, pull the trigger and—

We spot White on foot, casually walking from a bank, heading toward his truck.

The case agent and the squad supervisor quickly set up covert positions for the team. We need to take White down quickly and cleanly. White's used a handgun in prior robberies, so there's a strong chance he's armed right now.

For safety reasons, we want to get him before he reaches his truck. Car chases involving an armed felon are risky and usually don't end well.

White is looking around, to make sure he isn't being followed.

The case agent coordinates with the other officers and agents. My focus is on White, watching as he gets closer and closer to his truck.

Please let this go down smoothly.

The case agent gives the signal.

We move on White.

Take him by surprise before he can reach for his weapon.

The call goes out over the radio. "Subject in custody without incident."

The ability to bring closure is tremendously rewarding, the best and most important part of my job.

B.C. SANDERS

B.C. Sanders works as a police officer.

I'm thirteen years old, growing up in the South, skateboard-ing and listening to punk rock and hard-core music like Bad Brains. My brother and I are always very polite to adults, we don't get into trouble, so our mom gives us a lot of free-dom, lets us come and go as we please.

Skateboarding isn't allowed downtown, but we do it any-way. When the police chase me and my friends, we dash around the corner, toss our skateboards into dumpsters or trash cans, and then keep walking to blend into the crowds. The cops don't really know who we are, what we're wearing, or what we look like, so we never get caught. When the coast is clear, we double back to retrieve our skateboards from the trash and resume our skating.

My buddy drives a vintage milk truck with the names of bands like Black Flag and Minor Threat spray-painted on the sides. Kids think it's cool and come hang out with us. The cops pull us over a lot, thinking we're drug dealers.

We're not into drugs. I've never tried drugs, and I don't drink alcohol.

One time when we get pulled over, the cops examine the back of the milk truck and find our skateboards and bikes. One of the officers thinks we've stolen the bikes and starts butting heads with us.

"They're skaters," the other cop says to his partner. "They're good kids, they stay out of trouble. Let's cut them loose."

The encounter changes my perception of the police a bit. I've always considered them Robocops—automatons with no personality. This is the first time I've seen a cop as an individual.

I don't apply myself in high school and barely graduate. I get a job working in the tobacco fields. Some of my coworkers like to get high and drunk and often pass out on the job.

One of my slightly older coworkers pulls me aside and says, "Is that the future you want?"

"No."

"Do you have a plan?"

"A plan?"

"For life," he says. I know only a few things about the guy: he was in the Army, and he drives an immaculate truck. He's a hard worker, and he has a future. "What do you want to do with your life?"

I don't have an answer. I haven't put much thought into it.

"You need a plan," he tells me. "You need to find something you love and work for it, or you'll end up like those guys."

It gets me thinking. *I need to get myself squared away.*

I start reading a lot of books on Vietnam and Long-Range Reconnaissance Patrol (LRRP) units and, at seventeen, I decide to join the Army. There, I discover my passion: I want to get into law enforcement. Not the kind of cop who writes tickets or does a twelve-hour shift sitting in a parking lot eating donuts and drinking coffee. The kind who is responsible for protecting people from drug dealers and violent offenders.

I share my aspirations with my platoon sergeant.

"If you really want to be a cop, get the Army to pay for your college," he says. "And if you decide college isn't for you and want to come back to the Army, you can do that. We're not going to close up shop."

During my four years in the Army, I become very proficient with firearms and combat tactics. Now, I decide, I need to learn more about human behavior. As a cop, I'm going to be dealing with people all the time.

At twenty-one, I go to college to get a degree in psychology. It takes me five years. Because of my lackluster high school grades, first I have to take a year of remedial classes.

I approach my college classes the way I did everything in the Army—very disciplined and very regimented. I end up graduating in the top percentage of my class. I enter the police academy in my midtwenties.

The academy is very paramilitary. On top of staying physically fit and learning police policies, there are daily tests and quizzes on state and constitutional law. About forty percent of our class can't hack it.

*　　*　　*

I'm a new police officer, still in training, and sitting in the passenger seat of my patrol car late one night when my field training officer jumps behind the wheel. We take off in pursuit of an armed suspect who just robbed a fast-food restaurant in a city that borders ours.

"Guy with a red bandana stuffed the money in a pillowcase," he says, increasing speed. He's a former Marine, very intense. "The chief of police happened to be there, saw everything go down. When the guy ran away, the chief got in his vehicle and chased after him."

My heart rate spikes when my training officer starts driving against traffic.

"The suspect," I say. "Why is he coming here?"

"My guess is he's one of ours. A local. He's going to dump the car in a neighborhood he knows, so get ready."

We find the suspect and pull behind him.

He refuses to pull over.

"Get ready," my training officer says again.

We chase the suspect all over our district, blowing through intersections. The suspect ends up crashing into a telephone pole. There's a bright, nearly blinding flash, and then the whole block goes dark.

We come to a stop. As we get out of the car, my training officer says, "Watch out, we've got a downed power line."

We remove our sidearms and approach the car to clear it.

There's no one in the vehicle, but we find a pillowcase stuffed with cash—plus a firearm and a red bandana.

There's no sign of our suspect.

"Is it possible he could have run away?" I ask.

"After a crash like this? I don't see how. Maybe he got ejected from the car when it crashed."

Additional units arrive. We set up a perimeter and begin our search.

The suspect is nowhere to be found.

My training officer examines our dashcam, slows down the footage when he reaches the bright flash. Then I see it: a shadow of the suspect running across the street. We didn't see him because of the electrical explosion and because we were bringing our car to a full stop. The entire time, I'd figured he was still in the vehicle.

That night is my baptism by fire. I also learn an important lesson.

Never assume someone can't be violently ejected from a car, then get up, and still run away.

If you're a beat cop working in an area with a large gang or drug-dealing presence, you're going to be involved in a lot of foot pursuits. You quickly learn there's an art to it.

In the beginning, most cops think they can sprint and apprehend the suspect within three or four seconds. That rarely works out. You want to get on the radio fast enough to call out your areas because you want units en route to you as fast as possible.

A good beat officer makes an intense study of neighborhood terrain, including escape routes and shortcuts. While giving chase, he or she will make predictions over the radio. "Suspect is probably going to pop out on street A or street B.

I need two units. Give me one at A and one at B. Turn the lights on, let's get this perimeter blocked off."

To learn about gangs, the only option is to go straight to the source: the streets. I start building rapport with gang members. I keep conversations light, joke around and laugh.

"Your red bandana," I say to one guy. "Why do you wear it on the right side of your body?"

"Because we're East Side."

Gang members are big on hand signs. "What's this mean?" I ask one guy, showing him a hand sign a kid recently gave to me.

All the gang members laugh.

"*Damn,* dude," the guy says. "He threw a cop killer in your face!"

"What's up with *cop killer*? What does that mean?"

"He gave you the universal hand sign that says he wants to kill cops."

"*Oh,* so he's disrespecting," I joke. "Now why would he disrespect me like that? I'm the nicest dude on the beat."

Some of the members laugh. Over time, they teach me all the different hand signs they use. I practice them. I start cultivating informants.

I design classes to teach other officers about gang signs and initiations. How the gangs structure themselves and how they charge dues. Their lingo and how they code their text messages.

Each gang is different, as is each gang member. I apply my psychology degree to figure out why these guys do what they do. Some want a sense of family, others peer support. A very small fraction could be classified as having antisocial personality disorder—what people know as psychopaths. Someone absent of any sense of guilt and who can be very charming and manipulative and have no problem with violence—those men thrive in the gang world.

I'm walking up the street, responding to a 911 call from a man who is concerned about his elderly neighbor, a woman who has left her front door open—and is not answering her phone. The home is located in a tough, gang-infested neighborhood where I've responded to murders and shootings. I've chased dudes armed with assault rifles through these backyards.

A twelve-year-old kid is riding his bike. As I get closer, I see a police scanner bungee-corded to the bike's handlebars.

"Hey," he says. "Do you need a ten-seventy-six?"

Ten-seventy-six is police code for *Do you need another officer to assist with this call?*

"Ten-twelve," I say to him. *Stand by, I'll let you know if I need help.*

I check on the elderly woman. She's suffering from the flu, which is why she didn't answer the phone—and she had no idea she'd left her front door open. On my way back to my vehicle, I find the kid sitting on his bike, waiting for me.

I go over and start talking to him. He's got all of our ten-codes memorized.

"My grandmother bought me this police scanner," he says. "I'm going to be a cop one day."

It brightens my day, this kid wanting to do good in the world.

I see him a lot over the next few years. He's always listening to his scanner, showing up to crime scenes, watching what we do. I talk to him every chance I get. His family has had a lot of hardship. His brothers, sadly, got involved in criminal activity, but this kid is always upbeat. He's determined to go to college.

When he turns sixteen, he gets his license. I see him every now and then as he's driving to school, and we talk. A lot of really good things are happening in his life. He gets accepted to college, where he's decided to work in television production. When he graduates, he gets a job in Los Angeles.

We still keep in touch. The last photo he sent me shows him shaking President Obama's hand.

In sociological terms, that kid had every reason to join a gang. The cards were stacked against him. But his personality and what he wanted out of his life overpowered all that—and that really motivates me to keep connecting with kids like him, to keep doing this work.

JACKIE DEEN

Jackie Deen works in the Southwest.

"There's a guy swinging a machete in the parking lot at the Circle K."

Here we go, I think, staring at the police radio. *This isn't a mundane call.*

I'm behind the wheel of my police cruiser, my field training officer sitting next to me. I'm twenty-four, new on the job, and super, super nervous.

I tell dispatch we'll respond to the call, then hits the lights and sirens. I just hope I can get us to the convenience store.

It's late at night, I'm unfamiliar with the area, and navigation isn't my strongest skill. At the end of a recent midnight shift, my FTO told me to head back to the station. When I started driving in what I thought was the right direction, he asked, "Wow, you really don't want to go home tonight, do you?"

I get us to the Circle K. The place is brightly lit. Outside near the gas pumps, an older man, with long, greasy hair and clothes that look like they haven't been washed in days, is swinging a machete. People are in danger. We hop out of our cruiser, draw our guns on him, and order the man to get down to the ground.

Amazingly, he complies. We detain him. My FTO runs his license, finds out this person has an outstanding warrant for assault. We arrest him. He doesn't put up a fight as we put him in the cruiser and take him to jail.

The entire process is smooth and easy. Seamless.

I wish every interaction could go this way.

After my training period ends, I'm assigned to work the outskirts of the city, which are more rural. If something happens to me, my backups are usually far away.

CrossFit and my faith in God, especially, are good stress relievers for me. One of my friends gave me a wooden sign with my name carved in Hebrew letters. Jacqueline means "May God protect."

God is going to be with me, I keep telling myself as I respond to calls. *He's going to protect me.*

A lady calls on a Sunday at noon. There's a guy in her yard wearing jeans, sneakers, and a dirty white T-shirt. She asked him to leave, and he said, "I'll fucking kill you."

"Do you recognize this man?" dispatch asks.

"Yes. My son, John. He recently got out of prison."

"Does he live with you?"

"No. And I don't want him here."

The woman lives in a rural neighborhood where homes sit on one or more acres. I'm familiar with this area, and I don't see the man anywhere.

"My son just left," the mother tells me, and points to a winding dirt road.

That dirt road is an ATV path that leads south through the desert toward a major highway. I drive across the path, stopping when I spot a man wearing jeans, sneakers, and a dirty white T-shirt.

I park my car and glance at the map on the computer screen. If I get into trouble, all the backup units are a good distance away.

I get out, wave to the man, and say, "Sir, I need to speak with you."

He walks over. He's tall, almost six feet, and big. He probably weighs a hundred pounds more than me. I ask him his name. He says it's John, and then I ask him about the threatening conversation his mother described.

"I was just trying to get some food, but she wouldn't give me any," he says.

He turns to walk away.

I grab his arm. "You're not free to leave."

He jerks his arm away.

Starts running.

I chase after him. John runs up a little hill and trips. I tackle him to the ground.

He punches me in the face. I punch him back, as hard as I can, then I attempt to radio everyone in the area that I'm involved in a fight.

He tries to run away again. Again, I tackle him, and we continue to exchange blows.

Somehow, he manages to straddle me. As he repeatedly punches me in the face, all I can think about is my sidearm. *He's going to knock me unconscious and shoot me, shoot the next deputy he comes in contact with—maybe even return home and shoot his mom.*

In my earpiece, I hear warble tones—the signal for what's called a triple nine, an emergency alert to let the nearby deputies as well as the entire sheriff's department know that one of their own needs immediate assistance.

But I can't afford to wait. I've got to stop this guy now, before he kills me. I unholster my weapon, a 9mm Glock 17.

Point it at his face.

He knocks my Glock away as I squeeze the trigger, and in that moment, I have this weird sort of out-of-body experience where the gunshot sounds muffled, like I'm wearing ear protection, and I can literally see the bullet fly past his head and into the clear blue sky.

He tries to take the Glock away from me. I'm doing everything I can to hold on to it while trying to push him away with my free hand, my thoughts turning to a video I watched a couple of weeks ago about a female officer involved in a traffic stop.

A man pulled a weapon on her, and she begged for her life—*"Don't shoot me, please, don't shoot me."*—until her partner showed up and shot the guy.

That's not going to be me. I'm not going to let this guy get my weapon, I'm not going to be here begging for my life.

I hear a siren. For a split second, I think I'm imagining

it. Then John stops hitting me and looks up, searching the area.

"You don't want to do this," I say. "Just get off me—"

He's up on his feet, running. I holster my weapon, scramble to my feet. As I chase after him, I get on the radio. "We're running through the desert," I tell the responding units, giving them my location on the dirt road. "He's about to hit the highway."

I'm going to stop this guy, and I'm not going to stop until I get him.

Once I start something, I'm determined to finish it.

Another deputy pulls up onto the dirt road, directly in front of John. I take out my weapon. The other deputy is already out of his car, shouting commands.

John stops running, looks at the deputy—at me.

"Get on the fucking ground!" I scream.

John puts his hands up.

Gets on the ground.

After we detain him, I'm sent to the hospital. I've suffered a broken nose and some hematomas, but thankfully, that's the worst of it.

I'm told that, after my altercation, I ran nearly two hundred yards through the desert. I can't believe I ran that far. And while I was confident I would come out on top, there could well have been a different outcome.

But that reality doesn't stop me from doing my job. Being a police officer is a worthy cause. I believe in what I'm doing.

ADDY PEREZ

Addy Perez became a police officer after she left the Army. She works on the Community Action Team at a South Carolina sheriff's department.

I'm a new deputy and have just started working road patrols on my own when I'm told that a camera crew will be joining me on my Friday- and Saturday-night shifts.

Richland County, South Carolina, has been chosen as a setting for *Live PD*,[*] a TV show hosted by ABC's chief legal analyst, Dan Abrams, where on-duty officers respond to situations unfolding in real time.

The cameramen get inside my patrol car. As I'm driving, I

---

[*] *Live PD*, a reality show following officers on patrol, was one of A&E network's most successful series before it was canceled in 2020.

come to a stop behind a sedan waiting at a red light. I'm chit-chatting with the cameraman, when, out of nowhere, a red truck flies by me, going at least ninety miles an hour. It almost sideswipes both my vehicle and the sedan idling in front of me.

That driver could have killed us, I think as the truck blows through the red light.

I hit the lights and siren. When I catch up to the truck, he pulls over. I call for backup and exit my vehicle.

The driver's window is rolled down. A Hispanic male is sitting behind the wheel. The alcohol fumes coming off him are overpowering.

"Sir, you almost hit me. And you ran a red light. Why were you driving so fast?"

He looks at me, confused.

"I need your license and registration," I tell the driver.

He starts speaking to me in Spanish, his words slurred.

I answer the driver in Spanish, asking for his license and registration.

"I don't have a license," he replies in perfect English.

"If you don't have a license, then why are you driving?"

He doesn't answer. I ask him again for his registration. He gives it to me, reluctantly. I plug the information into my car computer, do a little digging, and come up with the driver's identity.

His name is Alex Rivera. This isn't the first time he's been pulled over for driving under the influence. He doesn't have a license because he lost it due to multiple DUIs.

The traffic unit that administers Breathalyzer tests isn't available, but that doesn't mean I can't arrest him. I head back to Rivera's truck.

"Sir, you're under arrest for reckless driving and driving with a suspended license."

"My family lives in another country. I need to work so I can send them money."

"Please step out of the car."

"Just listen to me, okay?"

Rivera keeps talking. I think about my cousin. I lost her to a DUI. She was in a car with a drunk driver who hit a barrier, sending the car off a cliff, and my cousin—who was about to become a registered nurse—was ejected from the vehicle and died.

When Rivera sees I'm not buying his sob story, he turns angry. "You don't know who my family is," he says. "You have no idea what I'm capable of."

He continues to threaten me, all in perfect English.

I arrest him, but Rivera won't let up. He refuses to accept the severity of the situation or the consequences of his actions. How his speed and carelessness could have killed me, maybe even the camera crew in my vehicle and/or whomever was in the sedan parked in front of me. How he might have hit and killed a pedestrian crossing a street.

After Rivera's booked, he goes to our jail facility, then into the court system.

He hires a lawyer. When his case comes up, his lawyer asks for a continuance, and gets one. It goes on for years, the lawyer asking for a continuance and the judge granting it. I know Rivera is hoping that his case will get dismissed or dropped.

It's not going to happen. I'm determined to make sure a judge hears this case, no matter how long it takes.

The COVID outbreak further delays Rivera's day in court. But when the day arrives, finally, four years later, Rivera is only charged with reckless driving. He's ordered to pay hefty fines and his license is permanently revoked, so he won't ever be able to drive legally.

But that doesn't mean he won't decide to get drunk again and illegally get behind the wheel.

Months later, my husband is out driving on the highway. His passenger is his best friend. A truck going one hundred miles per hour hits them. Two of the people I care about most.

My husband's car hits a barrier wall, spins out of control. It's a miracle they survive the crash.

The truck driver is a woman under the influence of narcotics. The highway patrolman who responds to the call finds CO_2 cartridges scattered all over the truck seat and floor. The cartridges, filled with nitrous oxide, are commonly referred to as whippets and provide a quick, cheap high.

Her license is revoked.

When I'm patrolling after midnight on the road, chances are that nothing good is going to happen, especially involving any person who gets behind the wheel after using drugs or alcohol.

If you do, you're not invincible. You're impaired.

Take a breather. Take a moment.

It's not just the DUI drivers we're concerned about. We're concerned about everyone. We're concerned about you.

JIM HERRING

Jim Herring joined the Army at eighteen and worked as an MP. At twenty-one, he became a police officer. He works in the South.

'm way out in the country, standing in front of a ranch house. Charlie, another officer, is with me.

Neighbors heard shots fired inside. They're worried about the woman who lives here. She's going through a divorce, and she's been drinking. They're concerned about a possible suicide.

The front door is locked. I look through the windows and see broken frames holding wedding photos. Every picture shows the same couple. Glass shards are strewn across the carpet.

I jump over the fence and gain entry through the back door, which leads into the kitchen. Charlie and I enter the house and split up to look for the woman. I find her inside a bedroom. I can only see the top of her head peeking out from the opposite side of the bed. She's crouched down on the floor, near a nightstand, sobbing uncontrollably.

I don't see a weapon, but I need to assume she has one.

I stand in the doorway. My sidearm is holstered.

"Hey, everything is going to be okay," I tell her.

"No, it's not," she sobs. "Everything's ruined."

"Nobody wants to hurt you."

"Everything's ruined," she says again. "Everything."

"No, it's not. No one is hurt, and no one here wants to hurt you. Do you have a weapon?"

She doesn't answer, just keeps crying.

We talk back and forth for a while. Sometimes she doesn't answer my questions. When she does, what she says doesn't make much sense because it's clear she's extremely drunk.

Supervisors arrive on the scene, wanting to know what's going on. I'm not leaving the doorway. I've gained a foothold, and I don't want to give it up and create a hostage/barricade situation, which will escalate things. As long as I can see her and talk to her, there's hope to resolve the issue.

I keep talking, easing myself closer to the bed, closer, looking for her weapon. I can't see it, but I'm assuming she has one.

The woman is looking over her bed, staring at the doorway. In the background, cops are trying to get in touch with her husband. We can hear their voices.

"It's going to be okay," I say again. "Trust me. I'm here to help you."

I've reached the foot of the bed. I step around the corner and see her—and the revolver gripped in her right hand.

"It's over," she says.

"It's not. Put the gun down—"

"You're wrong." She props the hand holding the revolver on her bed. The barrel is pointed in my direction. "It's over. Everything."

Her gaze shifts to me. "I'll just shoot you."

I don't draw my weapon so much as summon it, like it's an extension of my hand. It's all training and muscle memory. My sidearm is pointed at her, and with my other hand I reach forward and take away her weapon.

I holster my sidearm and throw her on the bed.

Handcuff her.

She passes out.

I have no idea what becomes of her. All I know is that she didn't die that night, and neither did I.

I still have no idea how my sidearm wound up in my hand.

JARED ARCENEAUX

Jared Arceneaux works in Louisiana.

People get into shootings all the time in Baton Rouge," says Lee, my field training officer. "This place is the Wild West. Anything can happen."

We get a "60 code 1" call—not an emergency, but more along the lines of a public service. A woman has called the sheriff's office about her husband, who was arrested on a domestic violence charge. He bonded out, and now he's headed home to pick up some clothing. She's requested officers be present.

"This will be a pretty run-of-the-mill call," Lee says. "Woman's going to want us to stand there so he doesn't attack her."

Lee is renowned as a badass dude, a real hard charger.

Before he became a cop, he did three combat tours in Afghanistan and Iraq. Lee's also on the SWAT team, which is where I want to be. SWAT's the reason I became a cop.

When I met Lee four days ago to start my training, the first thing he said to me was "Look, man. This is my ninth day in a row of work. They moved me to this shift so I can train you—and they're not paying me extra. I'm tired, you don't know anything, so shut the fuck up and pay attention."

I thought the dude was an asshole, but he's starting to warm up to me. We have some things in common, and I've shown him I'm not a complete and utter idiot. I'm pretty smart, well-spoken, and I can write a good report. Four days in, and he's no longer looking at me like I'm scum on his boot.

Dispatch comes over the radio with an update regarding our call. "Complainant just called 911," she tells us. "We can't understand what she's saying because she's screaming."

Lee hits the lights and siren. We arrive within minutes.

The home is a shotgun-style house, with a small carport area. The front door is ajar. As we run up the driveway, we see a man close the door.

"He's going to make a run for it," Lee says. "Cover the back."

I don't question him. During my training, Lee has told me that, in his experience, assailants in domestic violence events often flee when the police arrive because here in Louisiana, the law states that these perpetrators go *directly* to jail, no discussion.

I'm starting to jump the fence, to go into the backyard, when I hear a woman screaming and Lee yelling "Drop the knife!" from the other side of the house. I move away from the fence and bolt to the front of the residence.

The front door is open. It's been kicked in. *Lee must have done that. He heard the woman screaming, kicked down the door, and went in by himself.*

When I was at the academy, instructors played a video about Heraclitus, a Greek philosopher who ran a warrior-training compound. I remember Heraclitus saying something along the lines of "Out of every hundred men they send me, eighty are nothing but targets. The next ten shouldn't even be at the compound. Out of the remaining ten, nine are real fighters, and the last one will be a warrior. And we have to find the warrior because he'll be the one who brings the others back alive."

I want to be one of the top ten guys. Growing up, my dad always said, "You're either influencing or you're being influenced. Nothing is neutral." I've always taken that to heart, and now I'm being tested. Do I run to the danger, or run from it?

I unholster my pistol, move past the threshold, and step into a box-sized kitchen.

I hear a baby crying and Lee again shouting, "Drop the knife!"

Lee's about ten or twelve feet in front of me, his weapon aimed at a man standing behind a woman. The perp's got her in a choke hold, and he's stabbing her and stabbing her with a kitchen knife as he tries to back into a hallway leading into another room.

Lee doesn't have a clear shot, and neither do I. As I move around him, Lee fires five shots. The perp goes down. The woman slips from his grasp and falls to the floor.

I stare at the scene, stunned, as the baby continues

screaming from another room. *This is like something out of a Tarantino film.* I've never seen so much blood. The woman tries to get up but keeps slipping on the bloody floor. She's severely injured, her arms sliced up so bad she looks like she has pork chops hanging off them—and she has two knives broken off in her sternum.

The perp is locked in a death rattle.

Holy shit. He's dying.

The knife is on the floor, inches from the perp's hand. Lee kicks it away and says, "I've got to check the baby and the rest of the house."

The perp coughs up what looks like chunks of cranberry sauce. *What the hell is that? Is that from all the damage to his heart and lungs?*

Lee points to the woman. "Get her out of here and start working on her."

I move her outside and start working on her using the medical kit from the patrol car. I'm covered in her blood, skin, and adipose tissue (it looks like bacon grease) when EMS rolls up and takes over.

I don't think she's going to make it. She's lost way too much blood.

Command staff arrives. Someone gives me Clorox wipes to clean up. The captain has someone drive me home.

I'm covered in dried, crusting blood and pieces of skin and other things. My wife stares at me, horrified.

I've been a cop for four days.

My father became a cop when he left the Air Force, and my uncle was a detective. Growing up, I spent a lot of time around them and their partners and coworkers, listening to their stories. Their jobs sounded so cool, and right then I knew I wanted to be a police officer, too. A cop with integrity. If an officer doesn't have integrity, then the law doesn't have integrity, and then we don't have an organized society.

Cops involved in a shooting are put on a mandatory administrative leave while an investigation is conducted. During that time, I keep turning the event over in my mind.

I believe I did all the right things. Some cops, I'm told, feel guilty for *not* shooting, but I don't feel that way. I rendered aid to the victim, who, through the grace of God, has survived.

An innocent victim lived, and the good guys weren't hurt. And in the moment that mattered, I proved myself. I didn't screw anything up.

I couldn't ask for a better result. The incident is, from my perspective, very cut-and-dry, which probably explains why I don't lose any sleep over it.

My actions put me into a positive light with the department. Everyone wants to ride with me. I spend the next three months training with other FTOs. Six months later, I'm working a shift at a Walmart-sized parking lot shared by two nightclubs on a busy highway.

A lot of bad stuff goes down at that location, especially at this time of night when people are drunk. People get shot here all the time. One time a guy got his head chopped off by a machete.

Your first use of force as a cop is to make your presence known. You show up with your uniform looking good. You talk respectfully to everyone. The lot is packed with cars and well over two hundred people, everything lit up by blue police lights. It's 1:45 a.m.

I work the crowd with three other deputies; Lee, my lieutenant; and four armed security guards hired by the clubs. The atmosphere is charged, everyone on edge, wanting to get into their cars and drive away from here.

Pop.

A gunshot. I turn, drawing my pistol. People running everywhere, looking for cover.

I hear a second gunshot—this one much louder, the kind of noise a shotgun would make—and catch sight of a muzzle flash as I get low between two vehicles. I look over the front hood, see two dudes exchanging gunfire—one armed with a shotgun and firing at the second shooter, a guy wearing an oversized white T-shirt and baggy shorts. He's hanging out the side of a big white semitruck, shooting from an elevated position and using the door for cover.

The guy holding the shotgun gets hit as the deputies rush up behind him. They're ordering him to drop the weapon, and the guy in the truck is now shooting at the cops. The sheriffs and the armed security guys return fire as I work my way to the second shooter, using the cars for cover.

The shooter hasn't seen me yet.

I find a solid tactical position. I come over a car hood and, turning on my pistol light, yell, "Sheriff's office, drop the gun!"

The shooter turns to me and fires. I hear a bullet make a low, whizzing sound as it flies inches past my head.

If it had been a little to the left, my wife would be planning my funeral right now.

Oh, shit.

This is real.

I return fire, stop when he closes the door. I can't see him—and I have no idea who else might be inside the semi—but I hear more gunfire.

Then I hear an engine rumble to life. I take a quick look, see the truck driving out of the parking lot. The semi is shot to shit. It's not going to get far, not with all that damage.

There's no way I'm going to let the shooter get away.

The truck turns right, onto the highway. I reholster my weapon and sprint to my Crown Vic, where I've got a Remington 870 loaded with buckshot. *That will do the trick.* At thirty-five yards, a pistol is about as effective as a water gun. The shotgun is better at longer ranges—and more lethal.

I put the car in gear, about to pursue, when my lieutenant's voice comes over my radio. "Arceneaux, *stop.* You are *not* going by yourself."

I throw the car in park and then see him coming, hot on my heels. He jumps in the passenger's seat and grabs the shotgun.

I turn onto the highway. The semi has broken down two hundred yards away. As we pull up, a guy gets down from the truck. *It's the shooter, no question.* One leg is covered in blood. He's having trouble standing.

The lieutenant hands me the shotgun. I jump out and order the guy to drop to the ground.

The shooter takes off, his hands fumbling for something in the front of his shorts as he runs.

"Sheriff's office. Stop running and show me your hands!"

He ignores me. For a guy with only one working leg, he moves pretty fast. I take my finger off the trigger and chase after him with my shotgun shouldered, which slows me down.

No question this guy is a threat, but his back is toward me, and I can't see his hands. They're still in front of him. I don't know if he's holding a weapon or if he's trying to hold up his baggy shorts, to keep from falling.

An officer can shoot a fleeing felon if he or she is a danger to the public, but if you shoot someone in the back, you better have a *damn* good reason. You're going to have to articulate your actions and thought process later on, meaning, would a reasonable person, in the same situation, consider this felon a threat?

My mind counters, *Well, why do you think he's a threat? Do you see a gun?*

I'm not sure. As he runs, he keeps looking over his shoulder at me. Is he waiting for the right moment to shoot? For me to get closer?

If I pull the trigger, there's a good chance I'll kill him.

I don't know if I can live with the consequences.

I decide to give him a second chance.

I continue my pursuit, following him into a rental trailer facility off the highway. He dives under a U-Haul box trailer. I can see him clearly, but I still have no idea if he's armed.

He looks at me, knowing he's trapped. He puts up his hands and surrenders, but refuses to come out from underneath the U-Haul.

I hold cover, keeping the shotgun trained on him as he's handcuffed and patted down, after my lieutenant pulls him out.

The shooter isn't armed, and blood from a serious gunshot wound is squirting out from his leg. I run back to my car and grab a tourniquet.

I don't need it. EMS is already on the scene when I return, the shooter patched up. He's been hit three times, one critically to the leg.

In the aftermath, I learn that a group from Atlanta was selling drugs in the parking lot. The Baton Rouge dealers who work the lot got into it with them, and a fistfight broke out.

No one was shot tonight except for the two bad guys.

I still don't know how the hell that happened.

Four weeks after the incident, the dude who shot at me goes in front of the judge. The shooter is from Atlanta. He drove here with a friend who owned the semi. He's charged with two counts of attempted murder of a peace officer, which is a first-degree capital murder charge.

He gets out on a $10,000 bond.

I'm shocked. Stunned. All I can think about is the bullet that flew past my head.

This guy should have been held without bond. He could have killed me or someone else that night, and they let him go? They don't even hold him in state—he goes back to Atlanta, Georgia.

"Remember what I told you early on?" Lee says to me.

I nod. "A law enforcement officer is only as powerful as the justice system backing him."

"And you know the justice system here in Baton Rouge is notoriously weak."

It is. There are certain judges who are infamous for low-bond or no-bond cases. One judge had a guy on a weapons charge, and she commuted his sentence in exchange for him going out and committing *three acts of kindness*. The first thing he did once released was kill his girlfriend and their daughter.

And the woman who had almost been stabbed to death by her husband? That guy had been given the minimum sentence for his third felony conviction and was able to bond out for a few hundred dollars. He returned home and tried to kill her. Now she has permanent nerve damage and will never regain use of one of her arms. She's going to suffer a lifetime of PTSD.

I shouldn't be surprised my shooter walked away. I don't get a definitive answer, but my best guess is, because he's out of state, the city didn't want to pick up the tab for holding him here in jail for two years while he awaited trial.

In the days that follow, I have trouble sleeping. I turn hypervigilant, constantly examining and monitoring my surroundings. Because of the charges against the Atlanta shooter, my name is a matter of public record. This guy has a criminal history, mostly assault and dealing drugs, and while a small part of me wonders if he'll come back and pay me a visit, most of my mental energy is focused on wondering if he's going to hurt, possibly even kill, someone in Atlanta.

If I'd shot and killed him, would justice have been served? Maybe. But I'd be living with a different set of demons.

And I was *so close* to getting killed.

I find him on Facebook. He's using social media to sell weed. He makes light of the shooting, posts "I survived Baton Rouge."

I follow him online, praying that he doesn't hurt someone else.

The first incident involving the woman who was stabbed—I coped with that one well. With this one, not so much.

Nearly a year passes, and I'm still in a bad place mentally.

The department has created peer support groups where you swear an oath, saying, "I'm not going to tell the administration whatever you said," but everyone knows it's bullshit. *Someone* is going to talk. If word gets out about anything I say in the peer group, I'll be put on administrative leave, and no one will want to work with me.

I've seen it happen to coworkers.

If I seek out a different resource, like a therapist, I'm going to have to pay for it out of pocket—*and* keep it a secret. Another burden I'll have to carry.

I decide not to do anything. I internalize everything that's happened and put on a bravado performance. "I'm fine," I tell everyone. "Everything's good, thanks for asking."

Several years pass, and there are more tough moments, especially when I join SWAT. The Atlanta shooter is still free. It's unlikely his case will ever go to court.

I'm still trying to come to terms with that.

My work with SWAT makes me realize how I could have avoided a lot of that early mental suffering if I had picked up the phone, called a close buddy, and said, "Hey, bro, I'm struggling, and I need your help with this." We all want to be tough guys, but it's BS. That's why you have a SWAT team and not a SWAT guy. We all need each other.

LISSETTE RIVERO

Lissette Rivero worked in corrections before joining a police department.

The chief of police says, "I need you to come with me."

I follow him into a meeting room. He introduces me to Karl Williams, a detective who works in a city near Chicago. We all take a seat.

"A woman is alleging that a doctor sexually assaulted her," Williams says. "I did some digging into this guy. His name is Alvarez. He's from Peru and runs a popular medical clinic in a large Hispanic community. Nine years ago, a woman went to Chicago PD and complained that Alvarez sexually assaulted her at an appointment. For some reason, the case went nowhere."

I know where this is going, why I've been brought here.

After working patrol for five years, I was approached about the undercover world of special operations—with an emphasis on prostitution and human-trafficking casework, especially street and hotel stings. Would I be interested?

I said yes.

And I'm good at it. I'm sure I could have won an Oscar for some of my performances.

"Now two more patients have come forward," Williams says. "Both women are very wary about pressing any charges."

"Why?" I ask.

"Because they're illegal immigrants. My theory is the doctor is specifically targeting women who are illegal immigrants because he thinks they're too afraid to go to the police."

"And you want me to pose as a patient."

Williams nods. "The two female cops I work with, one is uncomfortable with the idea, and the other doesn't fit the criteria. I need someone who looks Hispanic."

I was born and raised in Chicago. I don't have any type of Latin accent, but I do speak Spanish.

"I'll do it," I say.

"You sure?"

"I've done everything else. Why not?"

I'm a single mom. I work eight-hour shifts, and when I do a nighttime sting, I hire a babysitter. The kids are little, know that I'm a cop, but they don't know about the other part of my job.

I arrive at the doctor's office wearing Daisy Duke shorts and a tank top. I've practiced my accent, and I've given a lot of thought as to how I'm going to play this.

I speak in Spanish to the woman who works the front desk. Then I'm taken to triage, where a nurse takes my vitals and asks me why I want to see the doctor.

Time to put on one of my Oscar-winning performances.

I start bawling.

"I'm very depressed," I say between sobs. "The INS took my son, and there's an arrest warrant out on me. I got arrested for stealing. I can't sleep at night because I'm so scared, my life is horrible, I—I just can't take it anymore. I want to kill myself."

"It's okay," the nurse says. "The doctor will help you."

I'm taken to one of the exam rooms. Several minutes later, the door opens. The man who enters is tall, with broad shoulders and a shaved head. He has kind eyes and a nice smile.

"Dr. Alvarez," he says, shaking my hand. He sits across from me. "Tell me how I can help you."

I need to convince him that I can't go to the police. I turn on the waterworks again and give the doctor the same song and dance I gave to the nurse.

He writes me a prescription for my depression. He hands it to me and asks me to stand. He tells me to turn around, and when I do, my eyes wet and puffy from crying, he puts his right hand on my shoulder.

His left hand holds a stethoscope. He places it under my left breast, to listen to my heart—which, obviously, is not the way you check someone's heart rate. He's doing this so he can inadvertently touch my breast with the back of his fingers. He's doing this because he knows that I won't run to the police.

He doesn't know I am the police.

He puts his arms around me and "cracks" my back. A spinal adjustment is a chiropractic technique, not typical of a general practitioner. He tells me to come back in four weeks. I head to the front desk, make another appointment, and then drive to the station to debrief Williams and the guys on his team.

"Alvarez's behavior is going to escalate," I tell them. "I've got to go to that next appointment, see what he does."

They agree.

I return for my second appointment, intentionally looking cute in a different tank top and a similar pair of shorts. I'm showing a lot of cleavage. I'm sitting on the exam table when Alvarez enters the room. I tell him the medication seems to be working, that I'm feeling better.

Alvarez is pleased. "I need to take your heart rate."

This time, he takes my breast out of my tank top. Then he places a hand underneath one breast and lifts it up a bit to listen to my heart.

I don't speak. I sit very still while he fondles my breast. Inside, I'm screaming with happiness.

Now I've got you. I've got you.

Dr. Alvarez tells me to make another appointment on my way out. He wants to see me in two weeks.

Detective Williams and his team are afraid Alvarez's behavior is going to escalate further, possibly to a more dangerous level. I don't need to go back. I was sexually assaulted twice, and both times I was alone with Alvarez. A nurse wasn't present.

They have enough to arrest him.

That weekend, the police hold a press conference. Over twenty women of Latin descent come forward. I'm asked to help interview them because they don't speak English. As I suspected, the women Dr. Alvarez targeted are all illegals. One of the women, I discover, was raped on an exam table.

I've arrested hundreds of men for soliciting prostitution and related offenses, but this one sticks out the most. Here you have a doctor, a supposedly trustworthy professional, who is sexually assaulting and raping women. What I'm not prepared for is the widespread disbelief and outrage.

Dr. Alvarez is a pillar of the community, residents say. He helps poor people. He gives free sample medications to patients who can't afford their prescriptions. If you can't pay for the doctor's visit, he won't charge you.

"Dr. Alvarez is a savior," they keep saying. "The police are lying."

The doctor keeps denying all charges. The case goes to court. When he sees me walk into the courtroom, the doctor realizes it's over. I know the truth.

SHAWN PATTERSON

Shawn Patterson works in the South.

I walk alone into the mayor's house.

I'm twenty-seven years old, the son of a preacher. When I was a kid, especially as a teenager, I got into all sorts of trouble. One of the cops knew my father and chewed my ass out.

Afterward, he took me on ride-alongs, out to lunch and dinner. We played football together. He tried to set my life on the right path, and that's when I realized, *Wow, cops are actually human beings with families and real emotions. They actually care about other people.* It kicked off a chain of events that led me into the police reserve program and now here, to the mayor's office.

After the mayor swears me in, I go back to the station,

where I'm given a badge. I'm officially one of two patrolmen in a four-man department watching over a little town with a population of less than five hundred. My sidearm, body armor, handcuffs, and uniform polo shirts—I have to pay for those items out of my own pocket.

We work in a small police department set inside a larger county. Our backups in neighboring towns can be anywhere from twenty to thirty minutes away, so we've got to be careful.

We get a late-night call about a stabbing at the Ross Mill Bridge. When we arrive, we see the glow of firelight.

Screams pierce the darkness. Not a single streetlight anywhere.

We take out our flashlights. I look over the side of the small bridge and see a bonfire near the riverbank. A guy lies nearby, in a fetal position. Another guy is standing over him, covered in a shocking amount of blood. Two young women are screaming for him to stop, to drop the knife.

My partner and I move down the embankment. The way the man and the women are acting and speaking—there's no doubt they're drunk. The guy holding the knife is a big, strapping dude. He refuses to drop his weapon.

We draw our handguns.

The guy is itching to get into a fight with us. We keep trying to de-escalate the situation, he keeps escalating it, and there comes a point where I think I'm going to have to pull the trigger.

Miraculously, he agrees to drop the knife. We kick it out of the way and apprehend him.

Three months later, I'm in court, testifying. The guy is now a defendant wearing a suit. His two kids are in the courtroom. That's when it hits me. *I'm twenty-six years old, and I almost ended this guy's life because he got in a drunken fight.*

The phone rings. It's two in the morning.

This isn't going to be good.

There's been an accident near the set of train tracks that comes through town. Two guys in a small pickup thought it would be fun to try to race the train and see if they could get ahead of it and jump the tracks.

Only it didn't work out that way. The train, going roughly forty-five miles per hour, hit the truck's driver's-side door, killing the driver and the passenger. I have to get down there and help secure the crime scene.

The truck looks like it ran over a land mine. Parts are scattered everywhere. The driver is dead.

The passenger is nowhere to be found.

When a train conductor hits the emergency brake, it takes about a quarter of a mile for the train to come to a complete stop. I look underneath the train and find what's left of the passenger's body. I call the detectives. After they finish processing the crime scene, we remove the body.

It's nasty.

The poor guy's lower torso is gone. One shoulder is gone, and he's missing most of his midsection. I move the beam of my flashlight underneath the train and the area around the tracks, saying, "Where's the rest of him?"

"Could be anywhere," a detective says. "Train hits a body, it just explodes. We're going to have to walk the tracks."

Everyone gets to work. I pair up with a detective. By 5 a.m., we still haven't found anything. We're all tired, frustrated, ready to go home.

The sun starts to come up. From the corner of my eye, I see someone up ahead waving to me. I turn, moving the beam of my flashlight, and see a hand waving at me as it runs up and down the tracks.

What in the world...

I turn on the flashlight's high beam.

A dog has gotten ahold of a severed arm.

I turn to the detective. "Are you seeing what I'm seeing?"

"Yeah. That's crazy. Really crazy." He sighs, shakes his head. "I guess we're going to have to deal with this."

The dog is running around like he's got a stick in his mouth and wants us to come play with him. We chase him down, yelling, *"Drop the arm!"* and of course the dog thinks it's a game and keeps running. Finally, he drops it, and all I can think is *I just had to chase and scream at a dog because it was trying to eat someone's arm.*

On the way home, I find a quiet place. I turn down the police radio and turn up my music.

In this job, I've seen a lot of messed-up shit. The badge, I've come to realize, doesn't make me impenetrable or better than anyone else. If anything, it makes me more responsible than anyone else.

But I don't feel responsible for the violent deaths of those two men tonight. I didn't ask them to race the train and try to jump the track. I didn't create that event, I just responded to it.

When I put it into that perspective, it makes it easier to process my thoughts and feelings. I know a lot of cops who deal with emotional, traumatic events and shut down. Turn hard. They lose their way, can't find their way back to their "normal."

I reach up for the visor and unclip a photo of my family. Holding the picture helps me navigate my way back to normal.

There's a big difference between a police officer and a cop. In the law enforcement community, they're called grass-eaters and meat-eaters.

Grass-eaters like writing tickets and working behind a desk. There's nothing wrong with that—you need both types—but I want to be the guy who's chasing a crackhead and out every night looking for drug dealers. That's where I feel I can really make an impact, which is why I decide to take a job in narcotics in a major Southern city.

The stuff that happens daily—date rapes, shootings, and murders—is devastating and never-ending. I was in the military, served overseas in Afghanistan and Syria. I felt safer over there than I do in some parts of this city.

I'm working as a field training officer, training a young recruit named Taylor, when a call comes over the radio for all supporting units to assist in locating and apprehending a female who has escaped the jail. She's been sighted in the southern part of the city. K9 units are out searching for her.

We set up a perimeter. Then we get reports that she's further south of our location.

What is she, a track star? How is she getting beyond the perimeters and the K9s?

I drive to a county road that's just outside the city limits. It's dark. In my headlights, I see a wrecked car in a ditch. Smoke is coming from the hood.

Did this escapee try to use this vehicle and take off? I call it in, describe the situation, then turn on the blue lights and get out to investigate.

Three men are running at full speed across the field, coming directly at us.

Taylor and I exchange "What's going on here?" looks.

Taylor is fresh out of a state law enforcement officers' training academy. The program is tough. A lot of people wash out. You've got to have a lot of grit to get through it—and Taylor, I can tell by his inner fire, is up to the task.

The three guys start screaming at us.

At the academy, you're taught to spread out. The last thing you want is to have two officers standing side by side in case someone pulls a weapon.

"Hey, hey!" I yell as I break away from Taylor, my hand unsnapping the leather hip holster for my sidearm. "Hold up. Let me see your hands, all of you, right now."

One guy stops running. "No problem," he says, putting up his hands.

"Get on the ground," I say.

He complies.

The second guy does, too. The third guy starts yelling, "Bitch got my car, bitch did this—"

"We'll figure out what's going on," I say. "First, let me see your hands, and get on the ground."

He reaches around his back and pulls a pistol from his waistband.

I bead down on him. *"Drop the weapon."*

He doesn't. He stands there, staring at me, while I scream at him again to drop the pistol. He hasn't pointed his weapon at me yet or made any furtive movements, but one wrong move and this guy is going to lose his life.

I don't want to kill this guy. I'm trying to find an escaped inmate.

"This is it," I say. "You move one more time, I'm pulling this trigger."

"Okay." He drops the pistol and gets on the ground.

"What the hell is your problem?"

"Man, I was just trying to let you know I had a pistol back there—and my bitch-ass girlfriend stole my car."

All three guys are on the ground. A backup unit is heading my way—

Taylor. Where is he?

I look around, see my training officer standing in the same spot where I left him. His hands are by his sides, and he's not holding a weapon. He's shaking like a leaf. I look him up and down—

His crotch is wet. I'm confused, and then it hits me.

He pissed himself.

I don't say anything. I don't want to embarrass him.

It turns out the woman who stole the car lying in the ditch isn't our escaped inmate. This guy's girlfriend did, in fact, steal his vehicle, wrecked it, and took off before he could chase her down. The dumbass boyfriend brought a pistol because he wanted to prove a point.

Three months later, Taylor gets out of law enforcement.

It gets me thinking about my time in Afghanistan and Syria. When I came home from overseas, I was able to leave behind the battlefields. There was something about having all that physical distance that allowed me to be able to flip a switch, tell myself, *That life, who I was over there—that was a whole other world. That life is behind me now. Now I have a new life.*

Cops don't have that luxury. We return to the same battlefields every day. Every day, no matter where I am, I see landmarks—the house where a three-year-old died. An apartment complex where a teenage girl was brutally raped by her boyfriend. A particular curb or block where someone, maybe a group of people, were shot and killed.

There's no escape.

On a Sunday night, a police officer observes what appears to be someone driving under the influence. The officer hits the lights and siren. Instead of pulling over, the owner of the vehicle decides to hit the gas.

Now the officer is involved in a pursuit. He puts the details over the radio.

I'm working on the interdiction/traffic unit, which covers everything from DUIs to interdiction on the highways. Because this is going to end up most likely being a DUI incident, I get involved in the pursuit.

It ends quickly. The driver crashes his car. Fortunately, no one is hurt.

The driver is still in his car when I arrive. He puts up a small struggle when officers remove him from the vehicle. They cuff him and put him in the back of a squad car. It's my job to interview him, see if he's drunk or high or both.

The offender is in his middle fifties, a scraggly, hippie-looking dude with white hair. He's sitting in the middle of the backseat of the cruiser, rocking back and forth, when I open the back door and start talking to him.

He doesn't respond. Keeps rocking and getting extremely irritated as he glares at the police partition, a Plexiglas divider that separates the front and back seats. The Plexiglas prevents spitting, and there's a slider that an officer can move so he/she can talk to the offender.

"Sir, you're going to need to—"

He violently headbutts a metal strip affixed to the slider on the partition. He splits his forehead right down the middle. Blood is running down his face and over his mouth. He's rubbing his lips together, glaring at me and refusing to speak.

Having a suspect go apeshit in a police cage isn't new. A lot of them try to injure themselves so they can go to the hospital instead of jail.

We call EMS, tell them we have a self-inflicted laceration to the head.

I return to the offender, open the door. "What the hell's your problem? What did you do that for?"

He leans his head back and spits blood all over my face. The blood gets into my eyes and mouth, and that's when I realize—the way he was rubbing his lips together, he was sucking blood into his mouth.

He looks at me, smiles. "Welcome to AIDS, motherfucker."

It's one thing to get shot in the line of duty or die in a car accident. But to die slowly of AIDS, your wife, kids, and family watching you deteriorate—I lose my cool.

It takes three officers to pull me off him.

EMS rinses my eyes and pulls off my clothes because they're covered in blood. I'm rushed to the hospital, where they immediately put me on a medical therapy called a triple—three antiretroviral medications combined into one pill that, more often than not, neutralizes HIV and some other blood-transmitted pathogens if they're treated in the early stages. I have to take one pill every day for seven days.

I spend the next week vomiting and waiting for my blood work to come back. By the end of the treatment, I've lost twenty pounds.

The offender's blood tests come back. He doesn't have HIV, but he does have hepatitis C. My blood tests come back negative, but that doesn't mean I'm in the clear. I'm going to need to get tested for the next six months.

It's pure hell, waking up every single day worrying if hep C is lurking somewhere in my bloodstream. I can't have unprotected sex with my wife. I know it can only be transmitted by blood-to-blood contact, but what if there's a small cut in my mouth that I don't know about, and I kiss my wife and give it to her? What if I get cut and accidentally infect my kids or my baby?

The offender goes to prison over the incident. I don't end up contracting hep C, thank God, but that year of mental anguish—it ends up taking a heavy psychological toll, especially when I'm at work.

Sometimes I act like an asshole.

When I served in the military, I wanted to make a difference. I wanted to serve my country, do something that matters—which is why I became a cop. Like many in law enforcement, I've gone through traumatic events that, at times, turned me hard. Made me rough around the edges and, at times, unapproachable. Behind every badge is a human being who has flaws and problems and suffers and is trying to do the best job he or she can.

TOM HAUSNER

Tom Hausner, a former Marine, works in Wisconsin.

It's my first night as commander of the SWAT team.

The 911 call comes from a woman in Minnesota.

"I was just on the phone with my girlfriend, Amanda Olson, who lives in your town. I was talking to her when she screamed, *'Oh, my God, he's got a gun!'* and then the line went dead.'"

Police are dispatched to Olson's address. She lives on the upper level of a two-story house that's been converted into two apartments. She doesn't answer her phone or the door, but police can make out someone moving behind the windows of her apartment.

It looks like a possible hostage situation. They call me, the SWAT commander, and ask for our assistance.

A true hostage rescue situation, the kind where you go in guns blazing, isn't common. You train for it, but the reality of it happening is very, very low.

I get word out to my guys, then speak to an officer at the scene. It's clear someone is in the apartment, I'm told, but the door is locked and no one is answering the phone.

When I arrive, the second-floor apartment appears quiet. But I see movement behind the curtains on the bottom level, which I'd heard was empty.

I turn to an officer and say, "I was told the bottom level was evacuated."

"It is."

"Well, someone's in there. We need to call that apartment, find out who it is."

When dispatch calls, a man answers and explains that the police took his wife to the station—but for some reason, they'd forgotten all about him.

"Sir, you need to get out of there," dispatch says. "Now."

An elderly gentleman comes out the front door. He can barely walk.

A city officer breaks cover to get to the man. I break my cover, too, get between the officer and the house. I provide cover as the officer puts the elderly man over his shoulder and runs away.

I set up a command post three blocks away and work on establishing communication with Olson. Someone is in there, moving inside the second-floor apartment. We have no idea if it's Olson or her kidnapper. My SWAT team negotiator keeps calling her landline, but no one picks up.

I have a good number of years and experience under my belt. My gut instincts tell me that we need to be careful.

My team is lined up, ready to deploy. "This is what we train for," I say, walking down the line and doing what's called a press check—tapping their chests to make sure they're wearing plates in their Kevlar vests. "This one's different. You need to be ready."

I set up my sniper team on a garage roof across the street. The sheriff joins me at the command post to monitor the situation.

Jeff, a SWAT team leader and a dear friend since we were kids, sets up his entry team on the right front side of the home. Swiftly but carefully, they get to work disconnecting the Christmas lights and the outside lights on the wrapround porch. If we cannot negotiate over the phone, we want to infiltrate the residence using stealth.

The front porch door for the apartment building is unlocked. If SWAT moves into the building, they'll have to take a steep stairwell to the second-floor apartment. None of our team has ever been inside this building before, so none of us has the first clue about the apartment's interior layout.

Jeff calls me at the command post. "There's a guy in here," he says. "He's performing a tactical peeking maneuver in the windows—looking out low one time, higher the next. He keeps mixing it up."

"What about the hostage?"

"Haven't seen her, just him."

My snipers report the same information.

Negotiators keep calling Amanda Olson's home number, but no one answers.

Then the guy inside the apartment yells out the side window. "Go away, I'm fine!"

This goes on for nearly two hours. He refuses to negotiate, to tell us who he is, or to let us talk to Amanda Olson.

At 11:07, Jeff radios me and says, "We can see him in the kitchen, and he's picking up a woman. She looks unconscious, like she's passed out or, possibly, dead."

My sniper team confers.

I think about the 911 call from Olson's friend. "Oh, my God, he's got a gun!"

Did this guy shoot her?

Is she bleeding out?

Does she have minutes to live, or is she already dead?

When I became a cop, I was young and dumb and would pray for the "big call"—the one where you puff out your chest and, like Superman, fly to the rescue and defuse a high-stakes situation, maybe even save someone's life.

Now I'm the one responsible for making the "big call." I'm responsible for sending these men, who are my friends, into battle—possibly right into the line of fire. And I have no idea what's waiting for them in there.

I take a deep breath. "Jeff, I know this is dangerous, but you guys are going to have to go in. And you're going to have to go now."

"Ten-four, hostage rescue."

The team enters the building in a "stack": Kirk, our scout and the number one man in the stack, is also one of the most experienced guys on my team. He tries the door.

It's locked.

Our breacher, Robbie, is at the end of the stack. He comes up to the front carrying the ram.

Jeff has set up diversionary flash-bangs in the back of the

house and sides of the house. When the devices go off, the hope is that they will divert the bad guy's attention from the front door while Robbie uses the ram to hit the door's locking mechanism. Once it's open, Kirk will throw a flash-bang into the room, and then the team will engage the target.

I'm at the command post when, outside, I hear the flash-bangs explode, followed by multiple gunshots.

My thoughts turn to the team. *Please, God, please let them be okay—*

I get on the radio to Jeff. "Are you clear? What's your status?"

"Negative!" Jeff screams in panic. *"Shots fired!"*

Thirty seconds pass. It feels like an eternity.

Jeff calls for rescue. *"Two down, shots fired."*

Two down.

He's talking about Kirk and Robbie.

My first job as SWAT commander, and I got my friends killed.

My expression gives away what I'm thinking. The sheriff looks at me and says, "You made the right call, Tom."

"I need rescue!" Jeff screams.

Anytime the shit hits the fan, my voice switches into a calm monotone. "Jeff, I know this is bad, but I need a status account. Tell me what's going on."

"We have an officer-involved shooting," Jeff replies.

Meaning, an officer has shot the suspect.

"Suspect is down," Jeff says. *"All officers accounted for."*

All officers accounted for... My men—my friends—aren't dead. They're *alive.*

The exhilaration I'm feeling is overwhelming. I high-five the sheriff.

*   *   *

I walk to the house, in the dark, one of my note-takers by my side. As I near the scene, I see Kirk and Robbie standing outside, in the street in front of the house. Their backs are facing me.

I'm so filled with emotion, the only thing I can say is "I'm glad you're okay."

They turn to me. Kirk is crying.

"I didn't want to shoot the son of a bitch," he says. "I didn't want to kill him."

I put a hand on his shoulder. "I know."

"I kept telling him to drop the gun."

"I'm glad you're okay."

Sometimes, it's the only thing you can say.

I look to Robbie. "Did you shoot, too?"

He nods.

"How many?"

"I don't know," he says. "A lot."

Robbie eventually walks me through what happened.

"It was a hollow-core door. The ram went through it, but the door didn't open—and that's when the bad guy opened fire. Jeff kept screaming, 'You've got to get through the front door,' so I hit it a second time. When it swung open, Kirk tossed a flash-bang inside the door, to the left of the room, where the shots were coming from, and went in. This is where it gets weird."

Robbie wipes his mouth on his sleeve. "Bad guy was lying on the floor, shoulder to shoulder with the hostage. He's on—"

"Shoulder to shoulder?"

Robbie nods. "He's on his back, lying right next to her, along with a good amount of ammo. He wouldn't stop shooting at us from the floor. Kirk and I fired multiple shots."

"The hostage?"

"Barely conscious. Bad guy shot her in the stomach well before we got here. Doc treated her. She's on the way to the hospital. Shooter, too. I don't think he's going to make it. He was riddled with entry and exit wounds."

I enter the house. All the evidence has been marked.

Two down, Jeff had said over the radio. He was referring to Olson and the shooter.

I check the kitchen and find blood everywhere.

This is where he shot her.

I return to the area a few feet from the front door, the place where the shooter lay down next to the victim and started firing at my men. A substantial amount of ammo sits on the floor. It's clear the shooter came to the apartment prepared for a gunfight. He knew we were outside—knew, at some point, that we were going to force our way in here—and then lay there, waiting to ambush us.

Blood tests will later reveal the shooter didn't have any drugs or alcohol in his system. But why did he bring Olson in from the kitchen and place her next to him? Was he hoping that, when the gunfire started, she would be accidentally shot and killed?

I'll never know. The shooter dies on his way to the hospital.

Olson is taken to surgery. Doctors find a bullet from the shooter near her spine. They can't remove it, but she survives.

Through the course of the investigation that follows, we learn that the man, it seems, had been infatuated with Olson. She rejected his advances, and at some point, he decided to take his revenge.

"If I can't have you," he told Olson before he pulled the trigger, "then no one can."

The shoot-out and hostage rescue are big news. We receive accolades.

Amanda Olson is invited to an award ceremony. This is the first time we're seeing her after the incident. It's rare to see the people we help after the fact.

She speaks about the events from that horrible night. How she was shot in her kitchen and had lost so much blood that she was sure she was going to die.

"Then I heard explosions," she says, looking at my men. "I saw you rush inside and right then I knew God had sent His angels."

DOYLE BURKE

Doyle Burke was studying engineering while working at a Kroger supermarket when he did a ride-along with a police officer. He left college and entered the police academy.

I'm at Myrtle Beach on a July family vacation, watching the end of a news clip. Susan Smith, a twenty-three-year-old mother of two, has been convicted of drowning her three-year-old and fourteen-month-old sons by strapping them in their car seats and then rolling her car into a lake.

When the newscaster says, "And in Dayton, Ohio, a similar case is proceeding," I straighten in my chair.

I work homicide in Dayton.

A four-year-old girl named Samantha Ritchie has been reported missing from her home in North Dayton. On the screen is a picture of a smiling little girl, hair in pigtails, wearing a long-sleeve white T-shirt printed with red and blue flowers.

Her mother, Jolynn, entered Samantha's bedroom, found it empty, and called 911. She told investigators that the bedroom window was open. She believes someone went through the window and abducted her daughter.

The story breaks to a news video. Jolynn is in her early twenties, with a round face and hair parted in the middle. One arm is in a white cast.

"I want my baby back!" she cries, massaging the cast with her other hand. "I just want my baby back."

She fidgets and looks around—anywhere but the cameras. Even though she's crying, there aren't any tears.

She's lying.

And her eyes... They're doll-like, absolutely lifeless.

I call my homicide partner. "Are we working this thing yet?"

"No, Missing Persons has it, but we think we're going to get it pretty soon."

The next day I get the call asking if I mind cutting short my vacation.

"No," I say. Because vacation was over for me once I saw that little girl's picture.

When I'm on a case, I get so involved that it becomes all-consuming. Intense. It's exciting to start with nothing and then move to the next step and the next until I get to that moment of "we're getting close now"—and it's always a team effort. Working homicide—we're not glory hounds. We're big on sharing any information we get with our troops. I don't have to be the one who breaks the case and carries out the arrest.

Jolynn Ritchie and her daughter live in a shit neighbor-hood full of drug dealers and pedophiles. A freeway overpass separates it from the old GHR Foundry. A lot of people who worked there back in the day said GHR stood for "go home and rest" because they worked you like a dog.

The foundry's buildings were razed, leaving twelve-foot-deep basements full of old, heavy equipment exposed to the elements. The rainwater and snow mix with oils, chemicals, and whatever else is down there, creating leaky pits filled with black toxic water. The place is pretty much a Super-fund site.

Because of the possible similarities to the Susan Smith case, Samantha's disappearance has created a media frenzy—all the major networks are there.

Armed with seven hundred volunteers and nearly thirty thousand flyers printed with Samantha's photo, we search the entire area for several days. We check out everything and ev-eryone. One guy we interview tells us, "I used to kind of mess around with Jolynn a little bit. How did you find me?"

"We're detectives," my partner says. "We do that kind of shit."

Jolynn's ex-husband—and Samantha's father—is Denton Ritchie. I know him well—we all do. Denton works as a janitor at the Dayton police department. A sergeant in the Army Reserve, he married Jolynn one month before he deployed. When he returned, he discovered his wife was addicted to crack cocaine. He got a divorce and petitioned for full custody.

We interview Denton. He's cleared quickly and then goes back out to searching for his daughter.

The search, all our work—we come up empty-handed. Homicide decides to borrow from another agency the best cadaver dog I've ever seen. The dog comes out, and ten minutes later stops at one of the pits and starts barking.

The summer day is as depressing as a day can get—overcast and raining. Humid. The water is so black there's zero visibility. We call the fire department. They arrive with pikes, which are basically big poles with hooked ends. A firefighter threads a pike inside the water and, a moment later, snags something on its hook.

When I started working homicide, I was at my first crime scene, staring at all the blood, the carnage and destruction, and said out loud, "Who does shit like this?"

One of the senior guys working with me said words I'll never forget. "When your life's shit, you do shit like this. Life doesn't have meaning to some people because they don't have a good life. They don't have anything to lose."

The fireman pulls out a body. I look at the victim's skin, waxy from days spent in the toxic water, the pigtails, the crushed skull, and I think of the picture of the adorable and smiling four-year-old running on every news station and fastened to every telephone pole in Dayton.

Why does shit like this happen?

There's nothing you can say.

"The victim's skull," I say to the pathologist. "Is it possible she could have fallen or something?"

He shakes his head. "That type of wound, you're definitely talking multiple blows."

Now it's official. We're dealing with a homicide.

My thoughts turn to Samantha's father, something Denton said when he was fighting for custody of his daughter. "It's a bad situation over there. Samantha needs to come live with me."

Denton searched for his daughter the moment he learned she was missing. On the second day of the search, without sleeping or eating, he collapsed.

"Maybe when Samantha is found," he told a friend, "I can finally get custody."

When I tell Denton the awful news, I see something inside him die.

To do this job, you've got to have a good home life, because if you don't, everything will just weigh on you.

One of my old partners had no real family, only his cop friends. When he retired, he said to me, "Man, I hope we stay in touch."

He was dead within a year.

Another guy I know who retired drank himself to death in a year and a half because he couldn't drink when he was working, and when you work homicide, you're working all the time.

Ernest Vernell "Vern" Brooks is forty-three and looks like a skeleton wrapped in skin. He's an ex-con and Jolynn's neighbor—and boyfriend.

We've already interviewed him a couple of times. Today, we're taking him downtown for another interview.

"We know a lot more than we did two weeks ago," I tell him. "A lot more."

"Like what?"

"We're going to tell you, but you'll feel better if you tell the truth."

Vern thinks it over. He's definitely nervous.

"I was there," he says, "but I didn't kill her."

Okay, here we go.

"Me and Jolynn were having sex on the basement steps when Samantha comes in. Jolynn got so mad she swung and hit Samantha with her cast. I think she was dead then. But Jolynn picked up a pipe wrench and beat her more. And so then she looked at me and she says, 'Get rid of the body or I'll blame it on you.' She knows I'm an ex-con. Who's going to believe me?"

"And then what did you do?"

"We wrapped up her body and went on over to the GHR."

Not much gets to me, I hate to say. I always tell people I wish I had more feelings. But carrying a wrapped-up lifeless four-year-old to an old, abandoned foundry in the early morning hours and dumping her in this twelve-foot pit of shit—and one of them is her *mother*?

Time to speak to Jolynn.

Police headquarters is connected to the jail by an enclosed skywalk. It's secure, allowing us to take prisoners back and forth. Police officers sneak Jolynn in through the jail, over the skywalk, because we need her to stay focused, not get distracted by the cameras gathered outside.

My partner and I stand on the third floor, looking down at the sea of media. Place looks like NASA with all the antennas and everything.

"If we don't get a confession out of her," I say, "we're

going to be working third-district midnights for the rest of our careers."

"After this one, I'll take that. I'll take that in a minute."

It takes a while, but finally she just says, "Look, this is what happened." Her story is very similar to Vern's.

We have our statement.

We also have a search warrant for the house.

One of my mentors once said, "When your crime scene is in a shithole, always look for the clean spots." When we go into the concrete basement, at the foot of the steps we see a newly painted part of the wall.

You've got to be kidding me. It can't be this easy.

When you're painting over blood, the paint is going to resaturate the blood. The evidence crew comes in, sprays luminol and uses an alternate light source. The painted area glows blue.

For blood.

The test results come back. The blood belongs to Samantha.

During the trial, Jolynn doesn't cry or flinch. When the prosecutor describes the murder, in graphic detail, and the last moments of Samantha's life, Jolynn shows no reaction, as though the prosecutor were describing the weather.

Denton Ritchie sobs into his hands.

The jury reaches a verdict in five hours and finds her guilty of every single charge brought against her. Denton Ritchie reads his victim impact statement. After he finishes, he turns to his former wife and says, "May God have mercy on your soul because I have none for you."

Jolynn is sentenced to life in prison. Vern, who agreed to

testify and pled guilty to three felonies—gross abuse of a corpse, tampering with evidence, and obstructing justice—gets five years.

Watching Jolynn being led away in handcuffs, I'm thinking how she's probably going to have the best time of her life in prison. Living there is way better than where she was living.

I think about Denton Ritchie working tirelessly to get custody of his daughter. In my mind, I keep hearing him say, "It's a bad situation over there. Samantha needs to come live with me."

The community really got behind this case more than any other I've ever worked—and I've worked some tremendously big cases. Everywhere I turn, there are billboards saying THANK YOU, DAYTON POLICE DEPARTMENT. Businesses put up signs saying, GOOD JOB, DPD.

I turn to my partner and, with a hint of sarcasm, say, "Good Lord, the community actually likes us."

"For now," he replies. "It's a good feeling, but it won't last."

DAVE MITCHELL

Dave Mitchell is a veteran of the Federal Bureau of Investigation.

Late Friday afternoon, as I'm getting ready to leave work at the FBI's New Orleans field office and enjoy a much-needed weekend with my family, I get assigned a lead from Jackson, Mississippi, about one of our federal fugitives, Henry Cook Salisbury.

"Little Henry," whose street name is linked to his short stature, is a member of the Dixie Mafia. The criminal group loosely based in the Deep South specializes in contract killings, armed robbery of jewelry stores and banks, and drug trafficking—including ripping off drug dealers. One of their most effective techniques is paying off public officials, including law enforcement.

Little Henry is a cut above the rest. Skillful and especially cruel. He's been criminally active for nearly fifty years—and arrested more than thirty times. Convicted in Georgia on multiple counts including attempted murder, he was serving a seven-year sentence when he escaped from the federal prison in Atlanta, Georgia.

No one has seen or heard from him since. He's a suspect in major crimes in the Southeast and East Coast.

The lead, I notice, is about a man named Harris Adams, an alleged associate of Little Henry's. Adams has recently been released from prison and, according to the lead, has been in contact with Little Henry.

The lead is marked as "routine," which means it's not urgent. I have a certain number of days to find Adams and interview him. But I see that the guy lives in a nearby apartment complex in Metairie, Louisiana, not far from the field office, less than forty minutes away.

Today, I'm carpooling home with Freddy, a fellow FBI agent who's also my next-door neighbor. I work on the violent crime squad. Freddy, a senior agent, has moved on to white-collar crime.

As I get into the car, I say to Freddy, "Would you mind coming with me to cover a lead? I want to get it out of the way."

"Sure, I'll come with you."

We talk about Little Henry during the drive.

"The lead," Freddy muses. "It came from Jackson, Mississippi?"

I nod, knowing where he's going. "The Gulfport FBI is actively investigating some corrupt public officials and law enforcement officers on the Gulf Coast. Officers with ties to the Dixie Mafia."

"Coincidence?"

"We'll see."

The apartment complex is in a nice suburb. It's early spring, the weather already on the warmer side. "I'll take the front," I say as we get out of the car. "You cover the back in case he decides to run."

I knock on the front door.

"Halt," I hear Freddy say from the back of the apartment. "Hold it, hold it right there."

When I move around to the back, I see Freddy has his pistol out, his attention pinned on a short, bald guy in a Hawaiian shirt.

"Where are you going, buddy?" Freddy asks.

The guy doesn't answer.

"Are you Harris Adams?" I ask.

He thinks about it for a moment, then nods reluctantly. The three of us go back into the apartment. Adams takes a seat on his couch.

"How come you ran from me?" I ask, my tone pleasant and respectful. When it comes to dealing with criminals, I always adopt the "good guy" philosophy. I don't get real tough on them. I treat them with professional respect and courtesy, try to get them to cooperate with me.

"Well, I'm a . . . Okay, look. I just got paroled, and I was afraid you guys were here to take me back," Adams says. My instincts tell me Adams isn't telling the truth, but I go along with it.

"Okay, that's good to hear," I tell him. "We're not here to jam you up, honest. I just want to ask you a few questions."

I take out a mug shot of Little Henry wearing thick black-framed glasses and a crisp white collared shirt. With his gray hair, Little Henry looks like an ordinary older businessman, maybe a youngish grandfather.

Adams examines the picture.

"I don't know this guy," he says.

"You sure? Because the information I have is that you work with him."

"You've got bad information."

"Then why'd you run out the back door?"

"I already done told you why. I do not want to go back to prison."

I try other avenues to get Adams to talk, trying to schmooze him, keeping up a gentle pressure, but he keeps insisting he doesn't know Little Henry. There's not much more than I can do, so I take the picture back and hand him my business card.

"You're not telling me the truth," I say. "If you have a change of heart, you can call me anytime."

I file my report on Adams and forget all about him. I'm working on a case out of New York involving two other fugitives who are a very hot priority.

In early May, I'm at my office desk when I get a collect call from Arizona.

The caller is Harris Adams. I accept the charges.

"Mr. Mitchell," he says. "That day you came to see me, well, I lied to you."

I keep my tone light. Conversational. "Well, why did you lie to me?"

"Because I was scared. I'd just gotten out of the penitentiary. I was there because I got in a fight and killed a couple of guys, but they let me out on good behavior."

I appreciate the honesty. "How about we start over?" I say.

"I've been a career criminal all my life. I know exactly who Little Henry Salisbury is. I know the FBI is investigating corruption on the Gulf Coast. I can help you there, too."

"Is that right?"

"Yes, sir. I know a lot of these players, the people you're looking for."

"Well, why are you calling me now?"

"Quite frankly, you're the first cop who's ever treated me decently."

Is this guy jerking my chain? "Okay. How about we start with Little Henry? Tell me what you know about him."

"I got arrested by the ATF over in Gulfport, Mississippi, and now I'm back in prison in Arizona. Come out here and interview me in person, and I'll tell you everything. You have my word."

"Unfortunately, the FBI doesn't work that way. There's a process. Procedures. There are agents in Arizona who will come out and talk to—"

"No," Adams says, adamant. "I'll only talk to you."

I see an opening. "Well, if you want me to come out there, you've got to give me something that shows me you're telling the truth."

"Little Henry's using the name Charles Smith," Adams says. "He's driving a white dually. You know what that is?"

I do. It's a six-wheel pickup truck used for towing.

"Right. He uses it to haul his trailer from trailer park to

trailer park. His dually's got a Louisiana tag, and Little Henry has a Louisiana driver's license. He travels all over the Southeast. He's involved in a lot of stickups."

"That's great information. What else can you tell me?"

He tells me the name of the chief of police in Gulfport.

"Little Henry," Adams says, "is in the process of taking a contract to kill him."

I go to my supervisor and tell him about my conversation with Adams. We take the information to the special agent in charge (SAC), who tells us to send the lead to our guys in Arizona.

Adams refuses to speak to them.

I decide to bend the rules a bit.

Keith, an agent and a good friend and mentor of mine, is a senior agent in Gulfport, Mississippi. I call and tell Keith that I have someone who can help him in his organized crime and corruption case—and help us find Little Henry.

Keith calls the US attorney in Mississippi, who files a legal document to have Adams removed from Arizona because he's willing to cooperate with the FBI. The Marshals Service transports Adams to a county jail in Jackson, Mississippi. On a Saturday, I drive over without telling my boss or anyone else.

Keith and I interview Adams together. Over the next five hours, he outlines the corruption happening in Gulfport and gives us specific details on the upcoming hit on the police chief.

"When's it going down?" I ask.

"I don't know an exact date," Adams replies, "but I hear it's very soon."

I've never had an informant give me so much credible—and incredible—information. I call my boss and tell him everything.

"This is great information. Let's get to work. We need to find this guy before he makes a move on the police chief."

Adams wasn't jerking my chain about Little Henry. I find a Louisiana driver's license for Charles Smith. He's in his early sixties now, and the picture looks nearly identical to Little Henry's mug shot.

The address on the license, I quickly discover, is worthless. But we have the vehicle registration for his white dually, and we know he's living in trailer parks. The question is, where?

We send the information out to the surrounding Southern states. Agents across the country drive to trailer parks, looking for a white dually.

It's like trying to find a needle in a haystack.

One June morning, I get a call from one of the surveillance agents, Grover, another former mentor of mine.

"We've got Little Henry," Grover says.

"You're kidding me."

"I'm at a trailer park right here in Slidell, Louisiana," Grover says. "I showed the park owner a picture of Little Henry and he says, 'That's Mr. Smith. He's renting the pad right down the road there. Pad number eight.' He's not here right now—he hasn't been here in a few days—but his trailer is still here."

I get off the phone and call a federal prosecutor to obtain a federal search warrant for his truck and his travel trailer. Then I gather five agents from my squad. We load up with shotguns. Little Henry is a very dangerous guy. He's been linked to several unsolved murders and contract killings, and there's no doubt in my mind that if this doesn't go down smoothly, he'll shoot it out with us to avoid going back to prison.

A light rain is falling when we meet up with Grover and another agent, Danny. We study the layout of the trailer park and come up with a plan.

Then we wait.

At five o'clock, we spot a white dually heading our way. He drives to the park entrance. As Little Henry pulls up, he's flanked by cars on each side so he can't escape. Before he can react, two agents from my squad, Don and Charlie, are already at the driver's-side door holding a shotgun and a pistol against the driver's ear.

Don and Charlie get Little Henry out of the truck, hand-cuff him, and find a nine-millimeter strapped to the fugitive's thigh. There's another loaded handgun in the truck.

I pull up to the truck and come face-to-face with Henry Cook Salisbury.

"Little Henry, you're under arrest for unlawful flight to avoid prosecution."

He doesn't say anything, but it's clear he's seething. He knows he's done, knows he's heading back to prison and never getting out.

We put him in the back of a car. I Mirandize him. I remove my weapon, hand it to one of the agents in the front of the car, then get in the backseat with Little Henry, who's now handcuffed.

I'm so excited and so nervous at having arrested one of the most dangerous guys I'd ever want to encounter.

"Would you like a cigarette?" I ask, removing a pack from my suit pocket.

Little Henry, an avid smoker, takes one without a word. I light it for him. I don't say anything as we drive.

Little Henry smokes, staring out the window as we cross the bridge over Lake Pontchartrain.

"You've been on the lam a long time," I finally say. My pad and pencil are ready. "What have you been up to?"

He ignores me.

"You owe me a little respect for catching you."

Henry turns and looks right at me.

He's going to talk.

"Fuck you," he says.

He turns back to the window. We continue to drive in silence for a bit.

"Hey, boy," he says. "How'd you catch me?"

"You know damn well I'm not going to tell you that."

More silence. His body, I notice, has relaxed a bit.

"Can I have another cigarette?" he asks.

I light another one for him. "Ready to talk?"

"You know I'm not going to talk to you."

He doesn't speak for the rest of the drive, remains silent when I book and fingerprint him.

After obtaining a federal search warrant for his trailer, we search it and find written diagrams of the chief of police's home and his mailbox. It appears Little Henry's plan was to plant a mail bomb using dynamite in the chief's mailbox.

The dynamite isn't in the trailer, but we find blasting caps, weapons, and ammunition—and every type of disguise imaginable. With all this evidence, along with the fact that

Little Henry is a convicted escapee from a federal penitentiary and a felon in possession of a gun, he's prosecuted quickly and returned to jail.

The Gulfport chief of police, it seems, is an honest man. The Dixie Mafia wanted him out of the way, which is why Little Henry took the contract to kill him.

The chief of police calls me at my office. "You saved my life. Thank you."

Hearing his voice, his words—it's humbling.

I receive calls from law enforcement officers from all over the Southeast and East Coast investigating crimes where Little Henry was a subject.

His arrest is very gratifying to everyone involved. A significant dangerous career criminal has been taken off the streets of America. Catching Little Henry, like any other fugitive, is a group effort.

The moral of the story, what I emphasize to new agents, is the importance of treating anyone you encounter, including career criminals, with respect. If I hadn't treated Harris Adams with respect and decency the first time I spoke with him, we would never have caught a bad guy like Little Henry.

JIM FOSTER

Jim Foster graduated from the United States Naval Academy and served overseas until he decided to join the "family business." His grandfather, father, and two younger brothers are all police officers in California.

S omething bad is happening in my neighbor's apartment," the 911 caller says. He gives the address and apartment number to the dispatcher. "I think there's a bunch of people in there doing dope, with children around. I can hear kids crying."

My partner and I take the call.

"Who is it?" a woman yells through the closed door when we knock. I immediately recognize her voice: Alice, a prostitute who works a stretch along the Pacific Coast Highway, where I patrol. I know Alice does dope, but she's not violent.

"Open up, Alice," I say after identifying myself.

"Do you have a warrant?"

"I know there are children in there. You have four seconds to—"

The door opens. Alice looks strung out. High.

"Oh, Mr. Foster," she says to me. "You don't want to go in there."

Razor blades cover nearly every surface of the apartment. People are smoking dope on couches, chairs, and the floor.

Three children under the age of four are sitting together on a sofa, their mouths covered in dried blood.

Alice knows me, and knows I'll take care of the kids. She tells me the dopers hit the kids when they cried, abused them in other ways, too. But she wants me to know she took no part in the awful things that happened in here.

Before we wrap the scene, we get another call, this one about a car roaring down the street at eighty miles per hour, bouncing off the curbs toward a busy intersection, then colliding domino-style into a line of cars stopped at a light before ricocheting off another vehicle, which drove head-on into a light pole.

The scene is a dangerous mess.

So is the driver. She wasn't drunk or high—she went into diabetic shock, which set off this chaotic chain of events.

While a witness, an older guy whose vehicle is pinned between the two wrecked cars, is telling me everything that happened, I'm still thinking about the kids from the apartment. Crimes against kids stick with cops, though each of us has to learn to suppress our reactions so we can do our job.

"It's a miracle I'm alive," the guy is saying. "I got out of my car and said a prayer. 'Thank you, Jesus, for letting me survive this.' That's when the light pole fell."

I look over at his Ford Explorer. It's crushed, completely totaled.

"That'll teach me to say a prayer before everything is said and done," he adds, shaking his head as if suddenly chilled. "I can't believe I got sucker-punched by Jesus."

I go back to patrolling the Pacific Coast Highway, see groups of addicts, prostitutes, and transients. I often stop and talk with them, get to know who they are and where they live. Some open up to me and share their life stories, how they arrived at these rock-bottom places in their lives. I try to help the best I can, and some folks assist me with information to help solve cases.

Talking with people who struggle with dependency has changed my thoughts on addiction. I've come to understand the unbelievable hold that heroin and cocaine have over them. These people can't stop themselves. And they've lost everything.

But they never had a great chance to begin with, either. Many grew up in families where education wasn't promoted, where the social norm was getting a beer at eleven at night. The generational attitudes they inherited are very hard to overcome.

From a block away, I hear a woman start howling.

Stay the fuck away.

It's Tiffany Hall, a woman I've arrested several times on multiple probation violations.

I stop to talk. I like Tiffany. She has a unique spirit. A lot of personality and a lot of humor, no problem saying it like it is. She has a tough outer shell but behind it is a soft inner person. She has a story to tell.

Everyone, I've come to realize, has a story to tell.

Tiffany grew up in a home constantly subjected to drug raids. She was taught to never trust the police. By the time she was fourteen, she had a child and was practically home-less. Her friends are gang members and addicts, and not only has she been stabbed and sexually assaulted multiple times, she's addicted to crack. I know the alleys where she goes to smoke—and sell—drugs.

For months, I've tried to get Tiffany to trust me a little more by encouraging her.

Tiffany, you're a nice person. You're funny. Tiffany, why don't you get help? Go back to school. This life you're living—it's horrible. You can do better than this.

Later that night, at two in the morning, I see a kid wandering the streets alone in a rough neighborhood. I pull over and ask him if everything's okay. He won't answer my question or tell me his name, only that he's thirteen.

I tell him I'm going to drive him home. He gives me his address. When we arrive, his parents are asleep.

"We knew he was out," his mother tells me, unhappy that I've woken her up. "He does this every day."

"How does he get home?"

She shrugs. "He just does."

"What's your son's name?"

"What name did he tell you?"

She isn't going to dime him off with his real name. She's loyal to him, but only supports his bad choices instead of parenting him, making sure he does the right thing.

This poor kid doesn't stand a chance.

*   *   *

My father is also a cop—a living legend in our department. When I was growing up, he'd share stories about his work at the dinner table. His guiding principle was "tough on crime, but kind to people."

I tell him about my encounters with Tiffany, about the kids abused by dopers, and the parents who don't care that their teenage son wanders the streets at night.

"Jimmy," my father says, "the world you live in, you think about how you're going to save up money, take the kids to Hawaii or wherever. You think about your kids' soccer games.

"To the people you encounter where you work," he points out, "that's fantasy. Their whole world centers around *How do I get my next beer?* and *Who's going to give me my next check? Am I going to be able to live in this apartment for three more months while I'm not paying rent because I've mismanaged my money or blown it on booze or drugs or a new phone?* Your concept of right and wrong, your values—these folks don't see that.

"To them, life is day-to-day survival."

My wife is a deputy district attorney. We share similar crime stories, but our realities are different.

"You work in an environment where all the dangerous predators are locked in cages," I've told her. "You get to direct when they're allowed out of their cages, when they're fed, everything. But I work on the savannah where there are no rules. All the dangerous predators are wild and free. It's scary."

In my line of work, some guys turn to booze. Some become

gym rats. I don't drink, which I've found to be a saving grace, so I put my energy into writing lesson plans. I teach at the academy.

Teaching is my therapy.

On the Fourth of July, my partner and I respond to a 911 about a naked man running down an alley with a young child, then entering a home belonging to his girlfriend's mother.

When we show up at the address, I find frantic neighbors surrounding two large men beating up a naked guy with baseball bats.

We break it up, start talking to people, and begin to piece together the puzzle as more police officers show up to help de-escalate the situation.

The naked man, Kenny, is loaded on PCP. When he'd run into the home and encountered his girlfriend's mother, the woman said, "I wish my daughter never dated you."

But Kenny, in his PCP-induced psychosis, hadn't even recognized the woman.

"You're one of them! One of the bad Russians who are trying to get me!" he'd said, attacking her. Kenny decapitated the woman. While her grandchild watched.

Tiffany shows up. The dead woman, I discover, is also *her* grandmother.

"You don't want to go in the house," I tell her gently. "Let us handle it. I promise, you don't want to go in there."

In that moment, something in Tiffany's face changes. I can tell she's learning that I sincerely care about her well-being.

I arrest Tiffany a few more times in the months that follow, but keep encouraging her to do better—that she *is* better.

Then Tiffany disappears. I can't find out where she went.

Did she move?

Is she in prison?

Did something bad happen to her?

"My next-door neighbor came over today with her son," a woman tells the 911 dispatcher. "She left him here and went back to her apartment to wait for her husband so they could talk about their divorce."

The woman takes a deep breath. "I hadn't heard from either of them, so I went over and knocked on the door. The husband answered, and he was just...he was very weird. And he had blood all over him. I'm worried something bad has happened."

I arrive at the duplex with several officers. I'm a sergeant now. Two officers go and talk to the woman who called 911. The boy, who's elementary school age, is still with her. The woman tells us she's sure no one has left the neighbor's apartment.

We go next door. As sergeant, it's my responsibility to quickly formulate a plan. When we force the door open, we find the husband lying on the floor, alive but covered in blood and holding a butcher knife.

He's been disemboweled.

And it looks pretty clear that he's done it to himself.

If that wasn't shocking enough, the man starts throwing his intestines at the two officers while screaming, "*If you come near me, I'll stab you!*"

We disarm the husband, then one of my officers climbs over him and moves into the neighboring bedroom.

The wife has been stabbed nineteen times. The officer drops to his knees and begins CPR, futilely hoping to save her.

It's a nightmare mess.

Over two hundred people gather outside the apartment complex, where the medical examiner is parked. A lot of kids and teenagers are mixed in the crowd, nearly every one of them holding an iPhone or an iPad.

They want to record the body bag being carried outside and then share the video with friends and post on their social media accounts.

My thoughts turn to the boy in the apartment. There's no doubt he'll have heard all the commotion, all our screaming and yelling. I'm sure he knows his father stabbed his mother. That his mother didn't make it, that his father is seriously injured.

I collect a bunch of bedsheets and we use them to make a wall from the front door to the back of the medical examiner's vehicle. The neighbors and other spectators boo us.

The locker room is the most powerful area inside the police department, the place where officers mentally unpack their day as they're taking off their guns and bulletproof vests. It's a Clark Kent type of thing—taking off your cape and putting on your glasses before you go home.

I share what happened. Talking with a few close guys can be like going to a therapist, minus the copay. The other advantage to talking with my peers is that they absolutely understand my emotions.

There was a time not that long ago that any cop who asked for help for stress or a mental health issue was in line for termination. In the last several years, mental health has become a destigmatized topic. Now departments are actively working to get an officer the help he or she needs.

But not everyone wants it. In less than two years, I've lost three friends to suicide.

A couple of days after the stabbing, I find out that one of the first officers who entered the apartment had been found by a neighbor bleeding outside on his front lawn. Though he'd been through other traumatic events over the course of his career, this was the first time a grisly crime scene bothered him so much he hadn't been able to sleep. While taking a shower to try and relax, he'd passed out from stress and exhaustion and fell through his glass shower door.

The officer gets help, but what happened at the apartment was the straw that broke the camel's back. He leaves our department and retires soon thereafter.

Months later, the second officer who rushed inside the apartment is involved in another brutal crime scene. A mother suffering from severe postpartum depression stabs her eight-month-old and then turns the knife on herself while the husband and their two-year-old son are asleep.

The mental health trauma is too much for the officer. He decides to quit the force.

Another cop lost. It's hard to explain to people the incredible emotional burden officers carry after enduring these types of incidents, especially when children are involved.

The City of Long Beach has been doing research into repeat criminal offenders who have stopped their lives of crime and found salvation.

I'm elated to find out that Tiffany Hall is one of these people.

"We interviewed her as part of our research," they tell me. "She shared her story and said you were instrumental in helping her change her life."

I'm just so glad to know she's alive.

Months later, the department invites me to a press conference. I'm now a lieutenant. I figure it'll be a sit-down interview with a reporter to talk about Tiffany's inspiring story. I'm surprised to find out that TV cameras will be there, along with a speech from the mayor.

Moments before the press conference is about to begin, I'm told Tiffany is also going to speak. We'll be meeting onstage, in front of a bunch of cameras and city officials.

It's a lot to take in.

After I give a short speech, Tiffany comes out of a back room, dressed in a sharp business suit. We smile when we see each other and hug. It's great to see her looking healthy and happy.

Tiffany takes the podium and introduces herself.

"I'm here because I want to thank Lieutenant Foster for his respect. And for his compassion. And for the empathy that he showed me and anyone he came in contact with."

She shares stories of how I encouraged her, how she listened to what I was saying and knew I was right, but her addiction was more powerful. After getting arrested, she tells the crowd, she used to sit in her cell and think about everything I told her. She surrendered and didn't look back.

Now she's clean and sober and about to receive her master's degree in social work. She works at a rehab facility. Best of all, she's fought hard to gain custody of her grandchildren from her son, who is having problems of his own. She's determined not to let them grow up in the same atmosphere she did.

Tiffany looks at me and, in front of the cameras, hands me an envelope. Inside is an invitation for her college graduation.

"I wouldn't miss it for the world."

Seeing Tiffany and what she's accomplished is one of the biggest joys of my professional life.

Three days later, I get a message to call a woman named Tracey. I remember the name. She was a drug addict and a prostitute. She disappeared, and I feared the worst.

"I saw you on the TV," Tracey says. "Do you remember me?"

"I do. How are you?"

She tells me she hit rock bottom a few years ago and decided to clean up her life. She now has a successful job. "I'm calling because I wanted you to know that Tiffany wasn't the only person you helped."

I think of what my father always said about being tough on crime but kind to people.

Kindness. Respect. Compassion. Empathy. You never know how these simple, small acts can help someone turn their life around.

WILLIAM SPRINGER

William Springer works as a part-time detective with the Palm Beach County Sheriff's Office.

I pick up the case file.

The victim's name is Rachel Hurley. On March 17, 1990—St. Patrick's Day—Rachel and a couple of her friends overnight on a boat near the Jupiter Inlet. When the boat docks near DuBois Park, at 2:45 p.m., the three girls head toward Carlin Park, where Rachel's mom is due to arrive at three.

Both parks are in Jupiter, a mile apart. Rachel's friends stop to use the restroom. Rachel doesn't join them. She doesn't want to be late. Rachel sprints down the beach and takes a shortcut through a wooded area.

She never arrives to meet her mom.

After an intensive search involving a hundred deputies, boats, a helicopter, and K9 units, Rachel's partially clothed body is discovered later that night.

Rachel Hurley was fourteen years old.

Two good detectives work the case and put in a lot of hard work, but no suspect emerges. In 2004, Rachel's case is picked up by the cold case squad, where I'm working as a supervisor. Together with the detective assigned to Rachel's case, we collect elimination DNA from people.

We get some good leads. I get excited by a few of them, but they don't pan out.

The detective works the case until he retires. I take it over full-time.

When I retire, Rachel's case is still unsolved.

Now I've come back out of retirement to work her case and other cold cases.

When it comes to DNA, most people don't realize that sensitive new kits are developed every couple of years that need even less DNA than the ones they're replacing. I go back to the evidence we collected from Rachel.

There's a new test called the M-Vac that uses vacuumlike suction on clothing to obtain any additional DNA it might retain.

Our cold case squad uses the M-Vac on the clothes belonging to an elderly female who, back in the early eighties, was suffering from dementia and accidentally wandered off from her home and was kidnapped. She was found unconscious on a dirt road, badly beaten and bleeding, her clothes and dentures scattered nearby. She was taken to the hospital and died eleven days later.

Serology redoes the late victim's rape kit. The DNA sample is placed into our state-run lab computer and comes back with a match. It belongs to a man who's been twice convicted of aggravated assault.

He also lives ten minutes from where the woman was allegedly kidnapped.

The confirmation process requires us to collect a saliva sample directly from a suspect. A detective secures a warrant, and when he arrives at the suspect's house to collect his DNA, the suspect keeps denying any involvement with the woman's kidnapping.

It's a match.

He's arrested.

On May 27, 1984, eight-year-old Marjorie "Christy" Luna leaves her home to walk to a nearby corner grocery store to buy cat food. She leaves the store and never returns home.

Police can't find a single trace of her. We get some good suspects, but we can't connect them to the case because we've never found her body, or any follow-up evidence.

On the thirty-fifth anniversary of her disappearance, we release a short documentary on social media, hoping for a new tip, information, anything. One tip we get is credible, maybe the most valuable lead we've ever received on her case.

Christy, we're told, played with a lot of little kids in the backyard of a nearby property the day she disappeared. The kids were setting out fireworks for Memorial Day, and through everything we've uncovered on her case, I can place her on that property that day.

Her body, we're told, is buried inside the home's septic tank.

The current owner of the house gives us permission to excavate. An anthropologist from Florida's west coast comes over and, along with her graduate students, they dig down to the septic tank. We block off the street, set up forensic tents, and spend a week working, sifting through the dirt, examining everything.

We don't find her remains.

A lot of people think cold case detectives should be making arrests every month. That's not the way cold cases work. The reality is, you can get a lead, think it's great, solid, and put in all the work—and then, *poof.* The reality is, you can work a case for years and never come up with a viable suspect. You hit a lot of dead ends.

You just have to keep working at it.

I use the M-Vac on Rachel's clothing.

Come up empty-handed.

It's disappointing, but tomorrow could be a better day. I won't know if I don't go back and try.

That's the way I always look at it.

In 1975, a woman is murdered in her house, sexually battered, stabbed to death, her throat slit—and we can't come up with a viable suspect. People tell me the husband did it, but he has a solid alibi.

Things were done differently in the seventies and eighties. Detectives didn't have computers or information stored on computers. I'm going back through paper receipts that were logged into evidence when an evidence technician says to me, "You don't have a complete list of all the evidence."

"What do you mean?"

"There's more evidence. You only got a partial list here."

I review the list and find out there's a rape kit I didn't even know we had. We process the kit, and the DNA matches a guy convicted of murdering a young girl in 1976. He's still alive and currently sitting on death row.

I go to death row to interview him. He admits to being in the area where the girl was murdered, but says, "I didn't murder her."

I tell him we're going to get a warrant to collect his DNA sample.

"Tell you what," he says. "When you get the test back, would you tell me what the results are?"

I tell him I will.

I sit down with him again and say, "The samples matched."

"I know," he says. "I did it."

"You knew the results would match. Why didn't you just tell me?"

"I like living on death row and don't want anything to screw that up."

He confesses to her murder—and to sexual battery.

"Why did you sexually assault her?" I ask.

"I thought she should have a little fun before I stabbed her to death."

My stomach feels like it's packed in ice.

We charge him for the murder. He pleads guilty and is sentenced to life—not that he was ever going anywhere.

Closing a cold case—it's an incredible high.

One day I just happen to answer the phone. The woman on the other end of the line is inquiring about a picture we recently put out on social media—the face of a young woman who was murdered in the eighties. We found only her skeletal remains, and a pair of penny earrings, and our forensic artist, using new equipment, managed to re-create what her face looked like in real life.

I've been trying to identify this Jane Doe for years. We figured out who was responsible for her death, but the suspect died—got himself murdered two days after he killed Jane Doe. Someone shot the guy and then set him on fire.

The woman believes the picture is her adopted sister. She starts describing her.

"Did she wear penny earrings?" I ask.

"Yes. Yes, she did."

We're able to identify the remains. It's her sister.

I give the woman her sister's penny earrings.

A high like that—it may be years before I get another one, but it makes all the prior years of work worth it.

I still get leads on Rachel. I follow them up and keep collecting elimination DNA, figuring someday I'll hit the jackpot. I'll get the right tip on Rachel if I keep her name out there. Maybe I'll get the right tip on Christy Luna, too. That would be great. I'll just keep plugging away.

I'll never give up.

ABOUT THE AUTHORS

James Patterson is the world's bestselling author. Among his creations are Alex Cross, the Women's Murder Club, Michael Bennett, and Maximum Ride. His #1 bestselling non-fiction includes *Walk in My Combat Boots, Filthy Rich,* and his autobiography, *James Patterson by James Patterson.* He has collaborated on novels with Bill Clinton and Dolly Parton and has won an Edgar Award, nine Emmy Awards, and the National Humanities Medal.

Matt Eversmann retired from the Army after twenty years of service. His first book with James Patterson was *Walk in My Combat Boots.*

Chris Mooney is the international bestselling author of four-teen thrillers. The Mystery Writers of America nominated *Remembering Sarah* for an Edgar Award. He teaches creative writing at Harvard.

For a complete list of books by
JAMES PATTERSON

VISIT
JamesPatterson.com

Follow James Patterson on Facebook
@JamesPatterson

Follow James Patterson on Twitter
@JP_Books

Follow James Patterson on Instagram
@jamespattersonbooks